Classroom Management Techniques for Students with ADHD

This book is dedicated to my wife, Jackie, and my two children, Jacqueline and Scott, who provide me with the love and purpose for undertaking projects that I hope will enhance the lives of others. My life has been blessed by their loving presence.

I also dedicate this book to my parents, who provided me with the secure and loving foundation from which to grow; my sister, Carol, who makes me smile and laugh; and my brother-in-law, George, who has always been a positive guiding light in my professional journey.

—Roger Pierangelo

This book is dedicated to my wife, Anita, and two children, Collin and Brittany, who give me the greatest life imaginable. The long hours and many years it took to finish this book would never have been possible without the support of my loving wife. Her constant encouragement, understanding, and love provide me with the strength I need to accomplish my goals. I thank her with all my heart. I also dedicate this book to my parents, who have given me support and guidance throughout my life. Their words of encouragement and guidance have made my professional journey a rewarding and successful experience.

—George Giuliani

A STEP-BY-STEP GUIDE FOR EDUCATORS

Classroom Management Techniques for Students with ADHD

ROGER PIERANGELO ~ GEORGE GIULIANI

Skyhorse Publishing

KH

Skyhorse Publishing books may be purchased in bulk at special discounts for sales promotion, corporate gifts, fund-raising, or educational purposes. Special editions can also be created to specifications. For details, contact the Special Sales Department, Skyhorse Publishing, 307 West 36th Street, 11th Floor, New York, NY 10018 or info@skyhorsepublishing.com.

Skyhorse® and Skyhorse Publishing® are registered trademarks of Skyhorse Publishing, Inc.®, a Delaware corporation.

Visit our website at www.skyhorsepublishing.com.

10 9 8 7 6 5 4 3 2 1

Library of Congress Cataloging-in-Publication Data is available on file.

Cover design by Michael Dubowe

Print ISBN: 978-1-63220-550-6
Ebook ISBN: 978-1-63220-967-2

Printed in the United States of America

9/23/16

Contents

Preface

I nattention, hyperactivity, and impulsivity are the core symptoms of Attention Deficit Hyperactivity Disorder (ADHD). A child's academic success is often dependent on his or her ability to attend to tasks and teacher and classroom expectations with minimal distraction. Such skill enables a student to acquire necessary information, complete assignments, and participate in classroom activities and discussions (Forness & Kavale, 2001). When a child exhibits behaviors associated with ADHD, consequences may include difficulties with academics and with forming relationships with his or her peers if appropriate instructional methodologies and interventions are not implemented.

When selecting and implementing successful instructional strategies and practices, it is imperative to understand the characteristics of the child, including those pertaining to disabilities or diagnoses. This knowledge will be useful in the evaluation and implementation of successful practices, which are often the same practices that benefit students without ADHD.

Research in the field of ADHD suggests that teachers who are successful in educating children with ADHD use a three-pronged strategy. They begin by identifying the unique needs of the child. For example, the teacher determines how, when, and why the child is inattentive, impulsive, and hyperactive. The teacher then selects different educational practices associated with academic instruction, behavioral interventions, and classroom accommodations that are appropriate to meet that child's needs. Finally, the teacher combines these practices into an individualized educational program (IEP) or other individualized plan—that is, a 504 plan—and integrates this program with educational activities provided to other children in the class.

Classroom Management Techniques for Students With ADHD: A Step-by-Step Guide for Educators is intended to provide educators with a step-by-step approach to the most effective methods of teaching students with ADHD.

Classroom Management Techniques for Students With ADHD: A Step-by-Step Guide for Educators was written to explain ADHD from the eyes of the teacher so that if a student in your class or school is diagnosed with this disorder, you can work effectively with the administrators, parents, other professionals, and the outside community.

We hope that *Classroom Management Techniques for Students With ADHD: A Step-by-Step Guide for Educators* will be helpful to you in understanding the key concepts of this disorder and understanding how to be an effective educator when working with students diagnosed with ADHD.

Acknowledgments

In the course of writing this book, we have encountered many outstanding professional sites. Those resources have contributed—and continue to contribute—enormous information, support, guidance, and education to parents, students, and professionals in the area of special education. Although we have accessed many worthwhile sites, we especially thank and acknowledge the National Dissemination Center for Children with Disabilities, the U.S. Department of Education, and the National Institutes of Health.

Both Dr. Pierangelo and Dr. Giuliani extend sincere thanks to Allyson Sharp and Laureen Shea for all of their hard work and dedication toward making this book a reality. We could not have completed it without your constant support and encouragement.

I (Roger Pierangelo) extend thanks to the following: the faculty, administration, and staff of the Department of Graduate Special Education and Literacy at Long Island University; Ollie Simmons, for her friendship, loyalty, and great personality; the students and parents of the Herricks Public Schools I have worked with and known over the past thirty-five years; the late Bill Smyth, a truly gifted and "extraordinary ordinary" man; and Helen Firestone, for her influence on my career and her tireless support of me.

I (George Giuliani) extend sincere thanks to all of my colleagues at Hofstra University in the School of Education and Allied Human Services. I am especially grateful to those who have made my transition to Hofstra University such a smooth one including Maureen Murphy (dean), Daniel Sciarra (chairperson), Frank Bowe, Diane Schwartz (graduate program director of early childhood special education), Darra Pace, Gloria Wilson, Alan Wenderoff, Laurie Johnson, Joan Bloomgarden, Jamie Mitus, Estelle Gellman, Joseph Lechowicz, Holly Seirup, Adele Piombino, Marjorie Butler, Eve Byrne, and Linda Cappa. I also thank my brother and sister, Roger and Claudia;

mother-in-law, Ursula Jenkeleit; sisters-in-law, Karen and Cindy; and brothers-in-law, Robert and Bob. They have provided me with encouragement and reinforcement in all of my personal and professional endeavors.

The publisher would also like to thank the following for their contributions to the book:

Mary Reeve
SPED Director
Gallup-McKinley County Public Schools
Gallup, NM

Sylvia Rockwell
SPED Professor
St. Leo University
Madison, FL

Anne Beveridge
Consultant
St. Paul Public Schools
St. Paul, MN

Mary Guerrette
SPED Director
Maine School Administrative District #1
Presque Isle, ME

West Keller
Special Educator
Social Skills Blended Kindergarten
McGilvra Elementary
Seattle Public Schools
Seattle, WA

About the Authors

Roger Pierangelo, PhD, is an associate professor in the Department of Special Education and Literacy at Long Island University. He has been an administrator of special education programs, has served for eighteen years as a permanent member of Committees on Special Education, has over thirty years of experience in the public school system as a general education classroom teacher and school psychologist, and serves as a consultant to numerous private and public schools, PTA, and SEPTA groups. Dr. Pierangelo has also been an evaluator for the New York State Office of Vocational and Rehabilitative Services and a director of a private clinic. He is a New York State licensed clinical psychologist, a certified school psychologist, and a Board Certified Diplomate Fellow in Student and Adolescent Psychology and Forensic Psychology. Dr. Pierangelo is the executive director of the National Association of Special Education Teachers (NASET) and an executive director of the American Academy of Special Education Professionals (AASEP). He also holds the office of vice president of the National Association of Parents with Children in Special Education (NAPCSE).

Dr. Pierangelo earned his BS from St. John's University, MS from Queens College, Professional Diploma from Queens College, PhD from Yeshiva University, and Diplomate Fellow in Student and Adolescent Psychology and Forensic Psychology from the International College of Professional Psychology. Dr. Pierangelo is a member of the American Psychological Association, New York State Psychological Association, Nassau County Psychological Association, New York State Union of Teachers, and Phi Delta Kappa.

Dr. Pierangelo is the author of multiple books by Corwin Press including *The Big Book of Special Education Resources* and *The Step-by-Step Series for Special Educators*.

George Giuliani, JD, PsyD, is a full-time, tenured associate professor and the director of Special Education at Hofstra University's School of Education and Allied Human Services in the Department of Counseling, Research, Special Education, and Rehabilitation. Dr. Giuliani earned his BA from the College of the Holy Cross, MS from St. John's University, JD from City University Law School, and PsyD from Rutgers University, the Graduate School of Applied and Professional Psychology. He earned Board Certification as a Diplomate Fellow in Student and Adolescent Psychology and Forensic Psychology from the International College of Professional Psychology. Dr. Giuliani is also a New York State licensed psychologist, and certified school psychologist and he has an extensive private practice focusing on students with special needs. He is a member of the American Psychological Association, New York State Psychological Association, National Association of School Psychologists, Suffolk County Psychological Association, Psi Chi, American Association of University Professors, and the Council for Exceptional Students.

Dr. Giuliani is the president of the National Association of Parents with Children in Special Education (NAPCSE), executive director of the National Association of Special Education Teachers (NASET), and executive director of the American Academy of Special Education Professionals (AASEP). He is a consultant for school districts and early childhood agencies, and he has provided numerous workshops for parents, guardians, and teachers on a variety of special education and psychological topics. Dr. Giuliani is the coauthor of numerous books by Corwin Press, including *The Big Book of Special Education Resources* and *The Step-by-Step Series for Special Educators.*

Step I

Reviewing Your Current Knowledge of Students With ADHD

Overview of ADHD

Attention Deficit Hyperactivity Disorder (ADHD) is a neurological condition that involves problems with inattention and hyperactivity-impulsivity that are developmentally inconsistent with the age of the child. This condition becomes apparent in some children in the preschool and early school years (National Institute of Mental Health [NIMH], 2006). We are now learning that ADHD is not a disorder of attention, as had long been assumed. Rather it is a function of developmental failure in the brain circuitry that monitors inhibition and self-control. This loss of self-regulation impairs other important brain functions crucial for maintaining attention, including the ability to defer immediate rewards for later gain (Barkley, 1998a). Behavior of children with ADHD can also include excessive motor activity. The high energy level and subsequent behavior are often misperceived as purposeful noncompliance when, in fact, they may be a manifestation of the disorder and require specific interventions. Children with ADHD exhibit a range of symptoms and levels of severity. In addition, many children with ADHD often are of at least average intelligence and have a range of personality characteristics and individual strengths.

ADHD was first described by Dr. Heinrich Hoffman in 1845. Dr. Hoffman, a physician who wrote books on medicine and psychiatry, was also a poet who became interested in writing for children when he could not find suitable materials to read to his three-year-old son. The result was a book of poems, complete with illustrations, about children and their characteristics. "The Story of Fidgety Philip" was an accurate description of a little boy who had ADHD. Yet it was not until 1902 that Sir George F. Still published a series of lectures to the Royal College of Physicians in England in which he described a group of impulsive children with significant behavioral problems, caused by a genetic dysfunction and not by poor child rearing—children who today would be easily recognized as having ADHD. Since then, several thousand scientific papers on the disorder have been published, providing information on its nature, course, causes, impairments, and treatments (NIMH, 2006).

Inattention, hyperactivity, and impulsivity are the core symptoms of ADHD. A child's academic success is often dependent on academic skills that enable a student to acquire necessary information, complete assignments, and participate in classroom activities and discussions (Forness & Kavale, 2001).

To acquire academic achievement, a child with ADHD faces a difficult but not insurmountable task of forming relationships. In order to achieve his or her full potential, he or she should receive help, guidance, and understanding from parents, guidance counselors, and the public education system (NIMH, 2006).

Prevalence of ADHD

ADHD is one of the most commonly diagnosed behavioral disorders of childhood (Gargiul, 2004). The disorder is estimated to affect between three and seven of every one hundred school-age children (American Psychiatric Association [APA], 2000). In the United States, an estimated 1.46 to 2.46 million children (Anderson, Williams, McGee, & Silva, 1987; APA, 2000; Bird et al., 1988; Esser, Schmidt, & Woemer, 1990; Pastor & Reuben, 2002; Pelham, Gnagy, Greenslade, & Milich, 1992; Shaffer et al., 1996; Wolraich, Hannah, Pinock, Baumgaertel, & Brown, 1996).

Although for years it was assumed to be a childhood disorder that became visible as early as age three and then disappeared with the advent of adolescence, the condition is not limited to children (Friend, 2005). It is now known that while the symptoms of the disorders may change as a child ages, many children with ADHD do not grow out of it (Mannuzza, Klein, Bessler, Malloy, & LaPadula, 1998).

Boys are four to nine times more likely to be diagnosed, and the disorder is found in all cultures, although prevalence figures differ (NIMH, 2006).

Causes of ADHD

ADHD is a very complex, neurobiochemical disorder. Researchers do not know ADHD's exact causes, as is the case with many mental and physical health conditions. As researchers continue to learn more about ADHD, scientists are making great strides in unlocking the mysteries of the brain. Recent technological advances in brain study are providing clues as to both the presence of ADHD and its causes (NIMH, 2006). In people with the disorder, these studies suggest that certain brain areas have less activity and blood flow, and that certain brain structures are slightly smaller in the prefrontal cortex, the basal ganglia, and the cerebellum (Castellanos & Swanson, 2002). These areas are known to help us inhibit behavior, sustain attention, and control mood.

ADHD has traditionally been viewed as a problem related to attention, stemming from an inability of the brain to filter competing sensory inputs such as sight and sound (Heward, 2006). Recent research, however, has shown that children with ADHD do not have difficulty in that area. Instead, some researchers now believe that children with ADHD are unable to inhibit their impulsive motor responses to such input (Barkley, 1997, 1998a; Pierangelo & Giuliani, 2006).

It is still unclear what the direct and immediate causes of ADHD are, although scientific and technological advances in the field of neurological imaging techniques and genetics promise to clarify this issue in the near future. Most researchers suspect that the cause of ADHD is genetic or biological, although they acknowledge that the child's environment helps determine specific behaviors (Pierangelo & Giuliani, 2007).

There is also strong evidence to suggest that certain chemicals in the brain—called neurotransmitters—play a large role in ADHD-type behaviors. Neurotransmitters help brain cells communicate with each other. The neurotransmitter that seems to be most involved with ADHD is called dopamine. Dopamine is widely used throughout the brain. Scientists have discovered a genetic basis for part of the dopamine problem that exists in some individuals with ADHD.

Scientists also think that the neurotransmitter called norepinephrine is involved to some extent. Other neurotransmitters are being studied as well (Castellanos & Swanson, 2002).

Imaging studies conducted during the past decade have indicated which brain regions may malfunction in patients with ADHD and, thus, account for symptoms of the condition (Barkley, 1998a). A 1996 study conducted at the NIMH (as cited in Barkley, 1998a) found that the right prefrontal cortex (part of the cerebellum) and at least two of the clusters of nerve cells known collectively as the basal ganglia are significantly smaller in children with ADHD. It appears that these areas of the brain relate to the regulation of attention. Why these areas of the brain are smaller for some children is yet unknown, but researchers have suggested mutations in several genes that are active in the prefrontal cortex, and basal ganglia may play a significant role (Barkley, 1998a). In addition, some nongenetic factors have been linked to ADHD including premature birth, maternal alcohol and tobacco use, high levels of exposure to lead, and prenatal neurological damage. Although some people claim that food additives, sugar, yeast, or poor child rearing methods lead to ADHD, there is no conclusive evidence to support these beliefs (NIMH, 2006; see also Barkley, 1998a; Neuwirth, 1994; NIMH, 1999).

Over the last few decades, scientists have come up with possible theories about what causes ADHD. Some of these theories have led to dead ends and some have led to exciting new avenues of investigation. The following is a summary of the possible causes of ADHD.

Environmental Agents

Studies have shown a possible correlation between the use of cigarettes and alcohol during pregnancy and risk for ADHD in the offspring of that pregnancy.

Another environmental agent that may be associated with a higher risk of ADHD is high levels of lead in the bodies of young preschool children. Since lead is no longer allowed in paint and is usually found only in older buildings, exposure to toxic levels is not as prevalent as it once was. Children who live in old buildings in which lead still exists in the plumbing or in lead paint that has been painted over may be at risk (NIMH, 2006).

Brain Injury

One early theory was that attention disorders were caused by brain injury. Some children who have suffered accidents leading to brain injury may show some signs of behavior similar to that of ADHD, but researchers have found that only a small percentage of children with ADHD have suffered a traumatic brain injury (NIMH, 2006).

Food Additives and Sugar

It has been suggested that attention disorders are caused by refined sugar or food additives, or that symptoms of ADHD are exacerbated by sugar or food additives. In 1982 the National Institutes of Health held a scientific consensus conference to discuss this issue. It was found that diet restrictions helped about 5 percent of children with ADHD, mostly young children who had food allergies. A more recent study on the effect of sugar on children, using sugar one day and a sugar substitute on alternate days, without parents, staff, or children knowing which substance was being used, showed no significant effects of the sugar on behavior or learning (NIMH, 2006).

In another study, children whose mothers felt they were sugar sensitive were given aspartame as a substitute for sugar. Half of the mothers were told their children were given sugar, and half were told that their children were given aspartame. The mothers who thought their children had received sugar rated them as more hyperactive than the other children and were more critical of their behavior (U.S. Department of Education, 2004).

Genetics

Attention disorders often run in families, so there are likely to be genetic influences. Studies indicate that 25 percent of the close relatives in the families of ADHD children also have ADHD, whereas the rate is about 5 percent in the general population (Pierangelo & Giuliani, 2007). Many studies of twins now show that a strong genetic influence exists in the disorder.

Researchers continue to study the genetic contribution to ADHD and to identify the genes that cause a person to be susceptible to ADHD. Since its inception in 1999, the Attention Deficit Hyperactivity Disorder Molecular Genetics Network has served as a way for researchers to share findings regarding possible genetic influences on ADHD (NIMH, 2006).

School Performance and ADHD

The school experience can be challenging for students with ADHD. Students usually are identified only after consistently demonstrating a failure to understand or follow rules or to complete required tasks. Other common reasons for referral include frequent classroom disruptions and poor academic performance (National Dissemination Center for Children with Disabilities [NICHCY], 2004).

Studies found that students with ADHD, compared to students without ADHD, had persistent academic difficulties that resulted in the following: lower average marks, more failed grades, more expulsions, increased dropout rates, and a lower rate of college undergraduate completion (Weiss & Hechtman, as cited in Johnston, 2002; Ingersoll, 1988). The disruptive behavior sometimes associated with the disorder may make students with ADHD more susceptible to suspensions and expulsions. A study by Barkley (1990b) and colleagues found that 46 percent of their student study group with ADHD had been suspended and 11 percent had been expelled (NIMH, 2006).

ADHD's core symptoms—inattention, hyperactivity, and impulsivity—make meeting the daily rigors of school challenging (Zentall, 1993). Difficulty sustaining attention to a task may contribute to missing important details in assignments, daydreaming during lectures and other activities, and difficulty organizing assignments. Hyperactivity may be expressed in either verbal or physical disruptions in class. Impulsivity may lead to careless errors, responding to questions without fully formulating the best answers, and only attending to activities that are entertaining or novel. Overall, students with ADHD may experience more problems with school performance than their nondisabled peers.

In the elementary years, ADHD usually causes these problems:

- off-task behavior;
- incomplete or lost assignments;
- disorganization;
- sloppy work or messy handwriting;
- inability to follow directions;
- errors in accuracy;
- inconsistent performance;
- disruptive behavior or spacey, daydreaming behavior; and/or
- social interaction difficulties.

Most of these problems continue around middle school and into high school and beyond. However, additional ones arise. That is because adolescents are expected to be much more independent and self-directed. They receive less supervision. Demands for concentration, more sophisticated thinking, and problem solving increase. ADHD makes it hard to meet those demands (NICHCY, 2004).

Given the additional problems that seem to arise in middle school and beyond, it is not unusual to see a student who has gotten by in earlier years dive academically around puberty (U.S. Department of Education, 2004).

The thinking difficulties associated with ADHD do not have to do with intellectual ability. Instead, they arise out of problems with concentration, memory, and cognitive organization. Typically, ADHD-related memory problems arise in two areas:

1. *working memory*, which helps the student keep one thing in mind while working on another; and
2. *retrieval*, which involves being able to locate on demand information that has been learned and stored in memory.

Many students also show problems in

- time management;
- prioritizing work;
- reading comprehension;
- note taking;
- study skills; and
- completing multistep tasks.

Clearly, a student with ADHD can have difficulty in any number of academic areas and with critical academic skills. Thus it is extremely important that the school and parents work together to design an appropriate educational program for the student. This program needs to include the accommodations, modifications, and other services necessary to support the student academically and promote successful learning and appropriate behavior (NICHCY, 2004).

Conclusion

The core symptoms of ADHD are developmentally inappropriate levels of inattention, hyperactivity, and impulsivity. These problems are persistent and usually cause difficulties in one or more major life areas: home, school, work, or social relationships. Clinicians base their diagnose on the presence of the core characteristics and the problems they cause.

Children with ADHD typically exhibit behavior that is classified into two main categories: poor sustained attention and hyperactivity-impulsiveness. As a result, three subtypes of the disorder have been proposed by the APA in the fourth edition of the *Diagnostic and Statistical Manual of Mental Disorders (DSM-IV)*: predominantly inattentive, predominantly hyperactive-impulsive, and combined types (Barkley, 1997). A child expressing hyperactivity commonly will appear fidgety, have difficulty staying seated or playing quietly, and act as if driven by a motor. Children displaying impulsivity often have difficulty participating in tasks that require taking turns. Other common behaviors may include blurting out answers to questions instead of waiting to be called and flitting from one task to another without finishing. The inattention component of ADHD affects the educational experience of these children because ADHD causes them to have difficulty in attending to detail in directions, sustaining attention for the duration of the task, and misplacing needed items. These children often fail to give close attention to details, make careless mistakes, and avoid or dislike tasks requiring sustained mental effort.

These characteristics affect not only the academic lives of students with ADHD, they may affect their social lives as well. Children with ADHD of the predominantly hyperactive-impulsive type may show aggressive behaviors, while children of the predominantly inattentive type may be more withdrawn. Also, because they are less disruptive than children with ADHD who are hyperactive or impulsive, many children who have the inattentive type of ADHD go unrecognized and unassisted. Both types of children with ADHD may be less cooperative with others and less willing to wait their turn or play by the rules (NIMH, 1999; Swanson, 1992; Waslick & Greenhill, 1997). Their inability to control their own behavior may lead to social isolation. Consequently, the children's self-esteem may suffer (Barkley, 1990a; Pierangelo & Giuliani, 2006).

Step II

Identifying Characteristics of Students With ADHD in Your Classroom

The principal characteristics of ADHD are *inattention, hyperactivity,* and impulsivity. These symptoms appear early in a child's life. *Because* many normal children may have these symptoms, but at a low level, or because the symptoms may be caused by another disorder, it is important that the child receive a thorough examination and appropriate diagnosis by a well-qualified professional (Pierangelo & Giuliani, 2006).

Symptoms of ADHD will appear over the course of many months, often with the symptoms of impulsiveness and hyperactivity preceding those of inattention, which may not emerge for a year or more. Different symptoms may appear in different settings, depending on the demands the situation may pose for the child's self-control. A student who "can't sit still" or is otherwise disruptive will be noticeable in school, but the inattentive daydreamer may be overlooked. The impulsive student who acts before thinking may be considered just a "discipline problem"; while the child who is well behaved but inattentive may be viewed as merely unmotivated. Yet, both may have different types of ADHD. All children are sometimes restless, act without thinking, or daydream the time away (Friend, 2005). When the student's hyperactivity, distractibility, poor concentration, or impulsivity begin to affect performance in school, social relationships with other children, or behavior at home, ADHD may be suspected. But because the symptoms vary so much across settings, ADHD is not easy to diagnose. This is especially true when inattentiveness is the primary symptom (National Institute of Mental Health [NIMH], 2006).

Subtypes of ADHD

There are three subtypes of ADHD:

1. Predominantly Inattentive Type

2. Predominantly Hyperactive-Impulsive Type

3. Combined Type (inattention, and hyperactivity-impulsivity)

Of course, from time to time, practically every person can be a bit absentminded, restless, fidgety, or impulsive. So why are those same patterns of behavior considered normal for some people and symptoms of a disorder in others? It is partly a *matter of degree*. With ADHD, these behaviors occur far more than occasionally. They are the rule and not the exception (Pierangelo & Giuliani, 2007).

Not all students have the same type of ADHD. Because the disorder varies among individuals, children with ADHD will not have all the same problems. Some may be hyperactive. Others may be underactive. Some may have great problems with attention. Others may be mildly inattentive but overly impulsive. Still others may have significant problems in all three areas (attention, hyperactivity, and impulsivity; National Dissemination Center for Children with Disabilities [NICHCY], 2004).

Inattention

Attention is a process. When we pay attention,

- we *initiate* (direct our attention to where it is needed or desired at the moment);
- we *sustain* (pay attention for as long as needed);
- we *inhibit* (avoid focusing on something that removes our attention from where it needs to be); and
- finally, we *shift* (move our attention to other things as needed).

Children with ADHD can pay attention. Their problems have to do with what they are paying attention to, for how long, and under what circumstances. It is not enough to say that a child has a problem paying attention. We need to know *where* the process is breaking down for the child so that appropriate individualized remedies can be created (Pierangelo & Giuliani, 2006).

With ADHD, there are three common areas of inattention problems:

1. sustaining attention long enough, especially to boring, tedious, or repetitious tasks;
2. resisting distractions, especially to things that are more interesting or that fill in the gaps when sustained attention quits; and
3. not paying sufficient attention, especially to details and organization.

These attention difficulties result in incomplete assignments, careless errors, and messy work. Children with ADHD often tune out activities that are dull, uninteresting, or unstimulating. Their performances are inconsistent both at home and in school. Social situations are affected by frequent shifts or losing track of conversations, not listening to others, and not following directions to games or rules (American Psychiatric Association [APA], 2000).

Children who are inattentive have a hard time keeping their minds on any one thing and may get bored with a task after only a few minutes. If they are doing something they really enjoy, they have no trouble paying attention. But focusing deliberate, conscious attention to organizing and completing difficult tasks or learning something new can be very problematic (NICHCY, 2004).

Homework is particularly hard for these students. They will often forget to write down an assignment or will leave it at school. They will forget to bring a book home or will bring the wrong one. The homework, if finally finished, is full of errors and erasures. Homework is often accompanied by frustration for both parent and child (NICHCY, 2004).

Children diagnosed with the Predominantly Inattentive Type of ADHD are seldom impulsive or hyperactive, yet they have significant problems paying attention. They appear to be daydreaming, "spacey," easily confused, slow moving, and lethargic. They may have difficulty processing information as quickly and accurately as other children. When the teacher gives oral or even written instructions, this child has a hard time understanding what he or she is supposed to do and makes frequent mistakes. Yet the child may sit quietly, and unobtrusively, and may even appear to be working but not fully attending to or understanding the task and the instructions (Pierangelo & Giuliani, 2006).

These children do not show significant problems with impulsivity and overactivity in the classroom, on the school ground, or at home. They may get along better with other children than those with the more impulsive and hyperactive types of ADHD do, and they may not have the same sorts of social problems so common with the combined type of ADHD. So often, their problems with inattention are overlooked. But they need help just as much as children with other types of ADHD who cause more obvious problems in the classroom.

Finally, it should be noted that many times when people refer to the child having ADD rather than ADHD, they are referring to the child with problems of inattention without the hyperactivity.

Hyperactivity

Excessive activity is the most visible sign of ADHD. Studies show that these children are more active than those without the disorder are, even during sleep. The greatest differences are usually seen in school settings (Barkley, 2000). Many parents find their toddlers and preschoolers quite active (Friend, 2005). Care must be given before labeling a young one as hyperactive. At this developmental stage, a comparison should be made between the child and his or her same-age peers without ADHD. Parents may report behaviors such as darting out of the house or into the street, excessive climbing, and less time spent with any one toy. In elementary years, children with ADHD will be more fidgety and squirmy than their same-age peers who do not have the disorder will be. They also are up and out of their seats more. Adolescents and adults feel more restless and bothered by quiet activities. At all ages, excessive and loud talking may be apparent (APA, 2000).

Hyperactive children always seem to be "on the go" or constantly in motion. In school, they may dash around and touch or play with whatever is in sight, or they may talk incessantly. Sitting still at dinner or during a school lesson or story can be a difficult task. They squirm and fidget in their seats or roam around the room. Or they may wiggle their feet, touch everything, or noisily tap their pencils. Hyperactive teenagers or adults may feel internally restless. They often report the need to stay busy and may try to do several things at once (NIMH, 2006).

Impulsivity

Children and youth with ADHD often act without fully considering the circumstances or the consequences. Actually, thinking about the potential outcomes of their actions before the fact often does not even cross their minds. Their neurobiologically caused problem with impulsivity makes it hard to delay gratification. Waiting even a little while is too much for their biological drive to *have it now* (NIMH, 2006).

The impulsivity leads these children to speak out of turn, interrupt others, and engage in what looks like risk-taking behavior. The child may run across the street without looking or climb to the top of very tall trees. Although such behavior is risky, the child is not so much a risk taker as a child who has great difficulty controlling impulse and anticipating consequences. Often, the child is surprised to discover that he or she has gotten into a dangerous situation and has no idea of how to get out of it. Some studies show that these children are more accident-prone, particularly those youth who are somewhat stubborn or defiant (Barkley, 2000).

Impulsive children seem unable to curb their immediate reactions or to think before they act. They will often blurt out inappropriate comments, display their emotions without restraint, and act without regard for the later consequences of their conduct. Their impulsivity may make it hard for them to wait for things they want or to take their turn in games. They may grab a toy from another child or hit when they are upset. Even as teenagers or adults, they may impulsively choose to do things that have an immediate but smaller payoff rather than engage in activities that may take more effort yet may provide a delayed but greater reward (NIMH, 2006).

Other Characteristics of Students With ADHD

Research is showing us that ADHD impairs the brain's executive function ability. It is as if the brain has too many workers but no boss to direct or guide them. When the brain's executive function abilities operate appropriately, we think, plan, organize, direct, and monitor our thoughts and activities (Pierangelo & Giuliani, 2006). In essence, our brain has a capable executive or boss.

Of course, none of us is born being our own executive. We acquire these skills as our brains develop and mature. Until we are able to monitor and regulate our own activities and lives, we rely on people and things outside of ourselves to guide and direct us. Puberty marks the time when we become increasingly "brain-able" to be our own boss.

Our executive abilities also help us to concentrate longer and to keep track of our thoughts, especially those we need later. We are less distracted by our own thoughts and find it much easier to return to work after we have been distracted (NIMH, 2006).

The brain's executive abilities also help us inhibit, or control, behavior. Inhibition is the ability to delay or pause before acting or doing. It allows us to regulate our thoughts, actions, and feelings. This self-regulation or self-control helps us manage or limit behavior. We learn to say "not now" or "not a good idea" to impulse. We learn to control our activity levels to meet situational demands. For example, to yell at a ball game is fine (unless we are shouting in someone's ear). Yelling in a classroom is usually not okay.

Thanks to our brain's executive abilities, we become driven more by intention than by impulse. That means we pause and reflect before we act. For instance, we are able to consider the demands of a situation along with the rules. We can delay an immediate reward in order to hold out for a later reward that is more meaningful.

With ADHD, the very brain areas responsible for executive function and inhibition are impaired. Children with ADHD can be considered hyperresponsive, because they behave too much. They are more likely to respond to events that others usually overlook (Barkley, 2000). Their characteristic disinhibition often causes others to find them annoying, irritating, or exasperating (Pierangelo & Giuliani, 2006).

Obviously, executive function difficulties can create distress and problems with daily functioning, including emotional control. In addition to symptoms of inattention, impulsivity, and hyperactivity, you may also see these types of executive function problems:

- weak problem solving;
- poor sense of time and timing;
- inconsistency;
- difficulty resisting distraction;
- difficulty delaying gratification;
- problems working toward long-term goals;
- low "boiling point" for frustration;
- emotional overreactivity;
- changeable mood; and
- poor judgment.

Self-Control and Self-Regulation Problems Seen in Students With ADHD—Are They a Matter of Deliberate Choice?

It is important to remember that the self-control and self-regulation problems seen in students with ADHD are not a matter of deliberate choice. These problems are caused by neurological events or conditions. People with ADHD know how to behave. They generally know what is expected in a given situation. But they run into trouble at the point of performance—that moment in time when they must inhibit behavior to meet situational demands. Their troubles may show up in how they act in the outside world or in their internal selves. They characteristically have inconsistent performance. This inconsistency is often mistaken for a lack of regard or respect, or as a lack of effort.

Because of inhibition problems, the disorder also makes it hard for the young person to follow the rules, especially if the rules are not crystal clear. Children with ADHD usually need a lot of incentive to follow the rules, too. That does not mean that they are intentionally being annoying or demanding. When a child's executive and control mechanisms are not functioning fully or normally, external incentives to pump up the child's ability to inhibit thoughts, feelings, and actions need to be provided.

Performance usually improves when external guides, rewards, and incentives are provided. These might include step-by-step approaches, extra praise and encouragement, and the chance to earn special privileges for better performance (NICHCY, 2004).

Problems Experienced by Children With ADHD Throughout the Life Span

ADHD is determined by the number of symptoms present and the extent of the difficulty these cause. Also the number of symptoms and the problems they cause may change across the life span. In a small number of cases, ADHD does go away in adolescence or adult years. However, in most cases, the problems shift. A hyperactive-impulsive fourteen-year-old may be able to stay seated longer than he or she could at age nine. While problems caused by hyperactivity-impulsivity seem to lessen with age, other ADHD-related symptoms usually become more problematic. For instance, demands for longer periods of sustained attention increase with age. So for example, even though a fourteen-year-old may sit still during a lengthy reading assignment, he or she may be bothered by an inability to concentrate.

The behaviors associated with ADHD change as children grow older. For example, a preschool child may show gross motor overactivity—always running or climbing and frequently shifting from one activity to another. Older children may be restless and fidget in their seats or play with their chairs and desks. They frequently fail to finish their schoolwork, or they work carelessly. Adolescents with ADHD tend to be more withdrawn and less communicative. They are often impulsive, reacting spontaneously without regard to previous plans or necessary tasks and homework.

Conclusion

Children with ADHD show different combinations of these behaviors and typically exhibit behavior that is classified into two main categories: poor sustained attention and hyperactivity-impulsiveness. Three subtypes of the disorder have been described in the *DSM-IV*: predominantly inattentive, predominantly hyperactive-impulsive, and combined types (APA, 2000). For instance, children with ADHD without hyperactivity and impulsivity do not show excessive activity or fidgeting, but instead may daydream, act lethargic or restless, and frequently do not finish their academic work. Not all of these behaviors appear in all situations. A child with ADHD may be able to focus when he or she is receiving frequent reinforcement or is under very strict control. The ability to focus is also common in new settings or while interacting one on one. While other children may occasionally show some signs of these behaviors, in children with ADHD, the symptoms are more frequent and more severe than in other children of the same age.

Although many children have only ADHD, others have additional academic or behavioral diagnoses. For instance, it has been documented that approximately one-fourth to one-third of all children with ADHD also have learning disabilities (Forness & Kavale, 2001; Robelia, 1997; Schiller, 1996), with studies finding populations where the comorbidity ranges from 7 to 92 percent (DuPaul & Stoner, 1994; Osman, 2000). Likewise, children with ADHD have coexisting psychiatric disorders at a much higher rate. Across studies, the rate of conduct or oppositional defiant disorders varied from 43 to 93 percent and anxiety or mood disorders ranged from 13 to 51 percent (Burt, Krueger, McGue, & Iacono, 2001; Forness, Kavale, & San Miguel, 1998;

Jensen, Martin, & Cantwell, 1997; Jensen, Shertvette, Zenakis, & Ritchters, 1993). National data on children who receive special education confirm this comorbidity with other identified disabilities. Among parents of children age six to thirteen years who have an emotional disturbance, 65 percent report their children also have ADHD. Parents of 28 percent of children with learning disabilities report their children also have ADHD (Wagner & Blackorby, 2002).

When selecting and implementing successful instructional strategies and practices, it is imperative to understand the characteristics of the child including those pertaining to disabilities or diagnoses. This knowledge will be useful in the evaluation and implementation of successful practices, which are often the same practices that benefit students without ADHD.

Step III

Understand the Legal Requirements for Identification of Students With ADHD

The process by which a child is found eligible for special education services is described within the federal law known as the Individuals with Disabilities Education Act (IDEA). The IDEA is the federal law under which schools

- evaluate children for the presence of a disability and their need for special services; and
- provide special education and related services to students who meet eligibility requirements.

Eligibility decisions about a child's need for special education and related services are made on a case-by-case basis. School districts may not arbitrarily refuse to either evaluate or offer services to students with ADHD.

In order for a child to be eligible for special education services, he or she must have a disability according to the criteria set forth in the IDEA or under state law (loosely based on IDEA). The disability must adversely affect his or her educational performance. Thus a medical diagnosis of ADHD alone is not enough to make a child eligible for services. Educational performance, which consists of social, emotional, behavioral, or academic performance, must also be adversely affected.

Presently, the IDEA lists thirteen categories of disability under which a child may be found eligible for special education. ADHD is specifically mentioned in the IDEA as part of its definition of "Other Health Impairment" (OHI).

IDEA's Definition of "Other Health Impairment"

In order to be eligible for special education, a student must meet the definition criteria for at least one of thirteen disability categories listed in the federal regulations. Some students may meet more than one definition. Many students with ADHD now may qualify for special education services under the OHI category within the IDEA. IDEA defines "other health impairment" as

> having limited strength, vitality or alertness, including a heightened alertness to environmental stimuli, that results in limited alertness with respect to the educational environment, that is due to chronic or acute health problems such as asthma, attention deficit disorder or attention deficit hyperactivity disorder, diabetes, epilepsy, a heart condition, hemophilia, lead poisoning, leukemia, nephritis, rheumatic fever, and sickle cell anemia; and adversely affects a child's educational performance. (34 Code of Federal Regulations §300.7(c)(9))

Section 504 and ADHD

If not found eligible for special education, students with ADHD may also receive special services be under Section 504 of the Vocational Rehabilitation Act. Section 504 is a civil rights law that prohibits discrimination against individuals with disabilities. Like IDEA, Section 504 requires schools to provide children who have disabilities with a free and appropriate public education. Unlike IDEA, however, which stipulates that a child has disabilities that require special education services, Section 504 identifies a qualified person as anyone with a physical or mental impairment that substantially limits one or more major life activities such as learning. This means that children who do not require special education are still guaranteed access to related services under Section 504 if the child is deemed to have an impairment that "substantially limits one or more major life activities" such as learning, and the school must try to adapt instructional methods to the needs of children with ADHD or ADD (Rabiner, 2006).

Since learning is considered a major life activity, children diagnosed with ADHD are protected under Section 504 if the disability substantially limits their ability to learn. If the child is eligible under Section 504, the school district must develop a Section 504 plan.

Section 504 provides a faster and more flexible procedure for obtaining some accommodations and services for children with disabilities and some children who are not eligible for services or protection under IDEA may receive protection. Thus Section 504 can provide an efficient way to obtain limited assistance without the stigma and bureaucratic procedures attached to IDEA (Rabiner, 2006).

The requirements and qualifications for IDEA are more stringent than those of Section 504 are. IDEA provides funds to state education agencies for providing special education and related services to children evaluated in accordance with IDEA and found to have at least one of the thirteen specific categories of disabilities, and who thus need special education and related services. ADHD may be considered under the specific category of OHI, if the disability results in limited strength, vitality, or alertness including a heightened alertness to environmental stimuli that results in limited alertness with respect to the educational environment and that is due to chronic or acute health problems (Friend, 2005).

Under IDEA, each public agency—that is, each school district—shall ensure that a full and individual evaluation is conducted for each child being considered for special education and related services. The child's individualized education program (IEP) team uses the results of the evaluation to determine the educational needs of the child (Gargiul, 2004). The results of a medical doctor's, psychologist's, or other qualified professional's assessment indicating a diagnosis of ADHD may be an important evaluation result, but the diagnosis does not automatically mean that a child is eligible for special education and related services. A group of qualified professionals and the parent of the child determine whether the child is an eligible child with a disability according to IDEA. Children with ADHD also may be eligible for services under the "Specific Learning Disability," "Emotional Disturbance," or other relevant disability categories of IDEA if they have those disabilities in addition to ADHD (Pierangelo & Giuliani, 2007).

After it has been determined that a child is eligible for special education and related services under IDEA, an IEP is developed that includes a statement of measurable annual goals including benchmarks or short-term objectives that reflect the student's needs (Heward, 2006). The IEP goals are determined with input from the parents and cannot be changed without the parents' knowledge. Although children who are eligible under IDEA must have an IEP, students eligible under Section 504 are not required to have an IEP but must be provided general or special education and related aids or services that are designed to meet their individual educational needs as adequately as the needs of nondisabled students are met (Friend, 2005).

Section 504 was established to ensure a free appropriate education for all children who have an impairment—physical or mental—that substantially limits one or more major life activities. If it can be demonstrated that a child's ADHD adversely affects his or her learning—a major life activity in the life of a child—, the student may qualify for services under Section 504 (Gargiul, 2004). To be considered eligible for Section 504, a student must be evaluated to ensure that the disability requires special education or related services or supplementary aids and services. Therefore, a student's ADHD does not interfere with his or her learning process may not be eligible for special education and related services under IDEA or supplementary aids and services under Section 504 (Pierangelo & Giuliani, 2006).

IDEA and Section 504 require schools to provide special education or to make modifications or adaptations for students whose ADHD adversely affects their educational performance. Such adaptations may include curriculum adjustments, alternative classroom organization and management, specialized teaching techniques and study skills, use of behavior management, and increased parent/teacher collaboration (National Dissemination Center for Children with Disabilities [NICHCY], 2004). Eligible children with ADHD must be placed in general education classrooms to the maximum extent appropriate to their educational needs, with the use of supplementary aids and services if necessary. Of course, the needs of some children with ADHD cannot be met solely within the confines of a general education classroom, and they may need special education or related aids or services provided in other settings.

Conclusion

Section 504 of the Rehabilitation Act of 1973 is a Civil Rights law to prohibit discrimination on the basis of disability in programs and activities—public and private—that receive federal financial assistance. The IDEA is an education act to provide federal financial assistance to state and local education agencies to guarantee special education and related services to eligible children with disabilities. While under IDEA, those protected are children ages three to twenty-one who are determined by a multidisciplinary team to be eligible within one or more of thirteen specific categories of disability and who need special education and related services. The major differences between IDEA and Section 504 are in the flexibility of the procedures. For a child to be identified as eligible for services under Section 504, there are less specific procedural criteria that govern the requirements of the school personnel. For individuals diagnosed with ADD, Section 504 and/or IDEA may play critical roles in their educational lives.

Step IV

Understanding the Evaluation Procedures Used in the Assessment of Students With ADHD

A diagnosis of ADHD is multifaceted and includes behavioral, medical, and educational data gathering. One component of the diagnosis includes an examination of the child's history through comprehensive interviews with parents, teachers, and health care professionals. Interviewing these individuals determines the child's specific behavior characteristics, when the behavior began, duration of symptoms, whether the child displays the behavior in various settings, and coexisting conditions. The American Academy of Pediatrics (AAP, 2000) stressed that since a variety of psychological and developmental disorders frequently coexist in children who are being evaluated for ADHD, a thorough examination for any such coexisting condition should be an integral part of any evaluation.

Behavioral Evaluations

Specific questionnaires and rating scales are used to review and quantify the behavioral characteristics of ADHD. The AAP (2000) developed clinical practice guidelines for the diagnosis and evaluation of children with ADHD and found that such behavioral rating scales accurately distinguish between children with and without ADHD. Conversely, AAP recommended not using broadband rating scales or teacher global questionnaires in the diagnosis of children with ADHD.

As with all psychological tests, child-rating scales have a range of measurement error. Appropriate scales have satisfactory norms for the child's chronological age and ability levels.

Collecting information about the child's ADHD symptoms from several different sources helps ensure that the information is accurate. Appropriate sources of information include the child's parents, teachers, and other diagnosticians such as psychologists, occupational therapists, speech therapists, social workers, and physicians. It is also important to review both the child's previous medical history and his or her school records.

Educational Evaluations

An educational evaluation assesses the extent to which a child's symptoms of ADHD impair his or her academic performance at school. The evaluation involves direct observations of the child in the classroom as well as a review of his or her academic productivity. Behaviors targeted for classroom observation may include

- problems of inattention such as becoming easily distracted, making careless mistakes, or failing to finish assignments on time;
- problems of hyperactivity such as fidgeting, getting out of an assigned seat, running around the classroom excessively, or striking out at a peer;
- problems of impulsivity such as blurting out answers to the teacher's questions or interrupting the teacher or other students in the class; and
- more challenging behaviors such as severe aggressive or disruptive behavior.

Classroom observations are used to record how often the child exhibits various ADHD symptoms in the classroom. The frequency with which the child with ADHD exhibits these and other target behaviors is compared to norms for other children of the same age and gender. It is also important to compare the behavior of the child with ADHD to the behaviors of other children in his or her classroom.

It is best to collect this information during two or three different observations across several days. Each observation typically lasts about twenty to thirty minutes.

In order to receive special education and related services under Part B of IDEA, a child must be evaluated to determine (a) whether he or she has a disability and (b) whether he or she needs special education and related services because of the disability. The initial evaluation must be a full and individual evaluation that assesses the child in all areas related to the suspected disability and uses a variety of assessment tools and strategies. As discussed in the section on legal requirements (see Step 3), a child who has ADHD may be eligible for special education and related services because he or she also meets the criteria for at least one of the disability categories such as specific learning disability or emotional disturbance. It is important to note that the assessment instruments and procedures used by educational personnel to evaluate other disabilities—such as learning disabilities—may not be appropriate for the evaluation of ADHD. A variety of assessment tools and strategies must be used to gather relevant functional and developmental information about the child.

An educational evaluation also includes an assessment of the child's productivity in completing classwork and other academic assignments. It is important to collect information about both the percentage of work completed as well as the accuracy of the work. The productivity of the child with ADHD can be compared to the productivity of other children in the class.

Once the observations and testing are complete, a group of qualified professionals (often referred to as the Committee of Special Education, Eligibility Committee, or Individualized Educational Program [IEP] Committee, depending on the state in which the child resides) and the parents of the child will review the results and determine if the child has a disability and whether the child needs special education and related services. Using this information, the child's IEP team, which includes the child's parents, will develop an IEP that directly addresses the child's learning and behavior. If the child is recommended for evaluation and determined by the child's IEP team not to meet the eligibility requirements under IDEA, the child may be appropriate for evaluation under Section 504.

Medical Evaluations

A medical evaluation assesses whether the child is manifesting symptoms of ADHD, based on the following three objectives:

1. to assess problems of inattention, impulsivity, and hyperactivity that the child is currently experiencing;

2. to assess the severity of these problems; and
3. to gather information about other disabilities that may be contributing to the child's ADHD symptoms.

Part B of IDEA does not necessarily require a school district to conduct a medical evaluation for determining whether a child has ADHD. If a public agency believes that a medical evaluation by a licensed physician is needed as part of the evaluation to determine whether a child suspected of having ADHD meets the eligibility criteria of the "Other Health Impairment" (OHI) category or any other disability category under Part B, the school district must ensure that this evaluation is conducted at no cost to the parents ("OSEP Letter," 1994).

In May 2000, the AAP published a clinical practice guideline that provides recommendations for the assessment and diagnosis of school-age children with ADHD. The guideline, developed by a committee comprised of pediatricians and experts in the fields of neurology, psychology, child psychiatry, child development, and education, as well as experts in epidemiology and pediatrics, is intended for use by primary care clinicians who are involved in the identification and evaluation process. The recommendations are designed to provide a framework for diagnostic decision making and include the following:

- Medical evaluation for ADHD should be initiated by the primary care clinician. Questioning parents regarding school and behavioral issues, either directly or through a previsit questionnaire, may help alert physicians to possible ADHD.
- In diagnosing ADHD, physicians should use *DSM-IV* criteria.
- The assessment of ADHD should include information obtained directly from parents or caregivers, as well as a classroom teacher or other school professional, regarding the core symptoms of ADHD in various settings, the age of onset, duration of symptoms, and degree of functional impairment.
- Evaluation of a child with ADHD should also include assessment of coexisting conditions such as learning and language problems, aggression, disruptive behavior, depression, or anxiety.

Conclusion

At present, no laboratory test exists to determine if your child has ADHD. You cannot diagnose ADHD with a urinalysis, blood test, CAT scan, MRI, EEG, PET scan, or SPECT scan, although some of these technologies are used for research purposes. Diagnosing ADHD is complicated and is much like putting together a puzzle. An accurate diagnosis requires an assessment conducted by a well-trained, licensed professional (usually a developmental pediatrician, child psychologist, child psychiatrist, pediatric neurologist, or clinical social worker).

The ADHD diagnosis is made on the basis of the observable behavioral symptoms. The symptoms of ADHD must occur in more than one setting. The person doing the evaluation must use *multiple sources of information*. Since symptoms of ADHD can also be associated with many other conditions, practitioners should never make a "snap diagnosis" either because a parent or teacher said he or she thinks the child has ADHD or because he or she has observed the child once. Children with ADHD commonly behave well on the first meeting. Furthermore, personal observation is only one source of a myriad of information.

Step V

Understanding How Students With ADHD Are Diagnosed

ADHD is considered a neurobiological disorder. Only a licensed professional such as a pediatrician, neuropsychologist, neurologist, or psychiatrist should make the diagnosis that a child, teen, or adult has ADHD. These professionals use the *Diagnostic and Statistical Manual of Mental Disorders, Fourth Edition, Text Revised (DSM-IV-TR)* as a guide (American Psychiatric Association [APA], 2000).

Over the last ten years, public awareness about ADHD has led to more children and adults being diagnosed with the disorder. Some people have expressed concern that the condition is being *overdiagnosed*. The American Medical Association (AMA) took a serious look into these claims. According to AMA's Special Council Report, however, there is little evidence of widespread overdiagnosis of ADHD or overprescription of medication for the disorder (Goldman, Genel, Bezman, & Slanetz, 1998).

Some parents see signs of inattention, hyperactivity, and impulsivity in their toddler long before the child enters school. The child may lose interest in playing a game or watching a TV show or may run around like a motor that does not stop. But because children mature at different rates and are very different in personality, temperament, and energy levels, it is useful to get an expert's opinion of whether the behavior is appropriate for the child's age. Parents can ask their child's pediatrician, a child psychologist, or a child psychiatrist to assess whether their toddler has ADHD or, more likely at this age, is just immature or unusually exuberant.

ADHD may be suspected by a parent or caretaker or may go unnoticed until the child runs into problems at school. Given that ADHD tends to affect functioning most strongly in school, sometimes the teacher is the first to recognize that a child is hyperactive or inattentive and may point it out to the parents and/or consult with the school psychologist. Because teachers work with many children, they come to know how "average" children behave in learning situations that require attention and self-control. However, teachers sometimes fail to notice the needs of children who may be more inattentive and passive yet who are quiet and cooperative such as those with the predominantly inattentive form of ADHD.

In order to be diagnosed with ADHD, children and youth must meet the specific diagnostic criteria set forth in the *DSM-IV-TR*, as discussed in Step 2. These criteria are primarily associated with the main features of the disability: inattention, hyperactivity, and impulsivity.

Symptoms Needed for a Diagnosis of ADHD

As mentioned earlier in this book, for a diagnosis of predominantly inattentive type of ADHD, six or more of the inattention symptoms must be present. For a diagnosis of hyperactive-impulsive type, six or more of the hyperactivity or impulsivity symptoms must be present. For a diagnosis of combined type, six or more symptoms of inattention, plus six or more symptoms of hyperactivity or impulsivity, must be present.

Often

The word *often* appears before each symptom of inattention, hyperactivity, and impulsivity in the *DSM-IV-TR*. In order to be considered a symptom of ADHD, a behavior cannot be "a once in a while" problem, nor can it be a problem that suddenly pops up. According to the *DSM-IV-TR*, the following must be true:

- There must be clear evidence of significant difficulty in two or more settings (e.g., at home, in school, with peers, or at work).
- Symptoms of inattention, hyperactivity, or impulsivity must be present at least six months.
- Some of these symptoms have to cause problems before age seven.
- The symptoms have to be developmentally inappropriate.

"Developmentally Inappropriate"

"Developmentally inappropriate" is an important point. If you look again at the symptom list for the three main features of ADHD, you will notice that some of these behaviors may be fairly normal at certain ages. For instance, no one expects a two-year-old to keep track of toys or to stay seated for very long. So losing things or not being able to stay in a chair for long would not be considered symptoms of ADHD at that age. These same behaviors in a ten-year-old, however, would be developmentally inappropriate. It is not expected for a ten-year-old to lose things constantly. A ten-year-old should be able to stay seated during one-half hour of class or a family dinner.

Professionals Who Make a Diagnosis of ADHD

Ideally, the diagnosis should be made by a professional with training in ADHD or in the diagnosis of mental disorders. Child psychiatrists and psychologists, developmental/behavioral pediatricians, or behavioral neurologists are those most often trained in differential diagnosis. Clinical social workers may also have such training.

The family can start by talking with the child's pediatrician or their family doctor. Some pediatricians may do the assessment with themselves, but often they refer the family to an appropriate mental health specialist they know and trust. In addition, state and local agencies that serve families and children, as well as some of the volunteer organizations, can help identify appropriate specialists.

Specialty	Can Diagnose ADHD	Can prescribe medication, if needed	Provides counseling or training
Psychiatrists	yes	yes	yes
Neuro-Psychologists	yes	no*	yes
Pediatricians or Family Physicians	yes	yes	no
Neurologists	yes	yes	no

*As of October 2006, Louisiana and New Mexico laws and regulations allow psychologists who have completed specific training and meet other requirements to prescribe psychotropic medications. The other forty-eight states and the District of Columbia allow only physicians to prescribe medications.

Knowing the differences in qualifications and services can help the family choose someone who can best meet their needs. There are several types of specialists qualified to diagnose and treat ADHD. Child psychiatrists are doctors who specialize in diagnosing and treating childhood mental and behavioral disorders. A psychiatrist can provide therapy and prescribe any needed medications. Child psychologists are also qualified to diagnose and treat ADHD. They can provide therapy for the child and help the family develop ways to deal with the disorder. But psychologists are not medical doctors and must rely on the child's physician to do medical exams and prescribe medication. Neurologists, doctors who work with disorders of the brain and nervous system, can also diagnose ADHD and prescribe medicines. But unlike psychiatrists and psychologists, neurologists usually do not provide therapy for the emotional aspects of the disorder.

Within each specialty, individual doctors and mental health professionals differ in their experiences with ADHD. So in selecting a specialist, it is important to find someone with specific training and experience in diagnosing and treating the disorder.

Lab Tests or Specific Medical Exams to Diagnose ADHD

At present, no laboratory test exists to determine if a child has this disorder. ADHD cannot be diagnosed with a urinalysis, blood test, CAT scan, MRI, EEG, PET scan, or SPECT scan, although some of these technologies are used for research purposes.

Formulating an "Accurate Diagnosis" of ADHD

Diagnosing ADHD is complicated and much like putting together a puzzle. An accurate diagnosis requires an assessment conducted by a well-trained, licensed professional (usually a developmental pediatrician, child psychiatrist, or pediatric neurologist). This professional must specialize in ADHD and all other disorders that can have symptoms similar to those found in ADHD. Until the practitioner has collected and evaluated all the necessary information, he or she can only assume that the child might have ADHD.

The individual doing the evaluation must use *multiple sources of information*. Since symptoms of ADHD can also be associated with many other conditions, it is problematic when practitioners make a snap diagnosis either because parents said they think their child has ADHD or because he or she has observed the child once. Children with ADHD commonly behave well on the first meeting. Furthermore, personal observation is only one source of information.

Recommended Diagnostic Procedure for Assessing ADHD

The AAP (2000) recommended that clinicians collect the following information when evaluating a child for ADHD:

1. A thorough medical and family history

2. A medical examination for general health and neurological status

3. A comprehensive interview with the parents, teachers, and child

4. Standardized behavior rating scales including ADHD-specific ones completed by parents, teacher(s), and the child when appropriate (know that people with ADHD typically are not great at accurately reporting symptoms of the disorder because it causes them to have poor insight into their own behavior)

5. Observation of the child

6. A variety of psychological tests to measure IQ and social and emotional adjustment; these tests also help to determine the presence of specific learning disabilities, which can co-occur with ADHD

Once the practitioner completes the evaluation, he or she makes one of three determinations:

1. The child does or does not have ADHD.

2. The child does not have ADHD but has either another disorder(s) or other factors that have created the difficulties.

3. The child has ADHD and another disorder (called a *coexisting condition*).

To make the first determination—that the child has or does not have ADHD—the clinician considers his or her findings in relation to the criteria of the *DSM-IV-TR* mentioned earlier.

To make the second determination—that the child's difficulties are caused by another disorder or other factors—the professional first considers the disorders that have symptoms similar to ADHD. Some mental health disorders have their onset after puberty, but early warning signs, which are very similar to ADHD symptoms, may be present. Thus it is possible for a diagnosis to change as the child develops and other disorders become more apparent. It is also possible for a child or youth to have more than one disorder, or co-occurring disorders.

Generally, the *DSM-IV-TR* requires clinicians to rule out ADHD if they see Pervasive Developmental Disorder (PDD), schizophrenia, and other psychotic disorders or if the symptoms are better explained by another disorder. For instance, although not very common, Bipolar Disorder (BPD) can be mistaken for ADHD in early years.

It is also true that major stressful life events can result in temporary symptoms that look like ADHD. Such events could include parental divorce, child abuse, death of a loved one, a move, or a sudden traumatic experience. Under these circumstances, ADHD-like symptoms may arise suddenly and, therefore, would have no long-term history. Remember, ADHD symptoms must exist for at least six months and cause some difficulty before the age of seven. Of course, a child can have ADHD *and* a stressful event, so such events do not automatically rule out the existence of ADHD.

To make the third determination—that the child has ADHD and a coexisting condition—the assessor must first be aware that ADHD can and often does co-occur with other difficulties, particularly learning disabilities, oppositional defiant disorder, and anxiety. A list of disorders that commonly co-occur with ADHD is provided in the following section.

The fact is that other mental health conditions such as those listed in the following can be the *result* of ADHD, *in addition* to ADHD, or *mistaken* for ADHD. That is why evaluations need to be conducted by a professional who is trained in a wide variety of child and adolescent disorders. Thorough and correct diagnosis is an essential first step to better treatments.

Disorders That Commonly Co-Occur With ADHD

Although these behaviors are not in themselves a learning disability, almost one-third of all children with ADHD have learning disabilities (National Institute of Mental Health [NIMH], 1999). Children with ADHD may also experience difficulty in reading, math, and written communication (Anderson, Williams, McGee, & Silva, 1987; Cantwell & Baker, 1991; Dykman, Akerman, & Raney, 1994; Zentall, 1993). Furthermore, ADHD commonly occurs with other conditions. Current literature indicates that approximately 40 to 60 percent of children with ADHD have at least one coexisting disability (Barkley, 1990a; Jensen et al., 2001; Jensen, Martin, & Cantwell, 1997). Although any disability can coexist with ADHD, certain disabilities seem to be more common than others are. These include disruptive behavior disorders, mood disorders, anxiety disorders, tics and Tourette's Syndrome, and learning disabilities (Jensen et al., 2001). In addition, ADHD affects children differently at different ages. In some cases, children initially identified as having hyperactive-impulsive subtype are subsequently identified as having the combined subtype as their attention problems surface.

Oppositional Defiant Disorder (ODD)

Oppositional Defiant Disorder (ODD) is a pattern of negative, hostile, and defiant behavior. Symptoms include frequent loss of temper, arguing (especially with adults), refusal to obey rules, intentionally annoying others, and blaming others. The person is angry, resentful, possibly spiteful, and hypersensitive.

Conduct Disorder (CD)

Conduct Disorder (CD) is a pattern of behavior that persistently violates the basic rights of others or society's rules. Behaviors may include aggression toward people and animals, destruction of property, deceitfulness or theft, or serious rule violations.

Anxiety

Anxiety is excessive worry that occurs frequently and is difficult to control. Symptoms include feeling restless or on edge, easily fatigued, difficulty concentrating, irritability, muscle tension, and sleep disturbances.

Depression

Depression is a condition marked by trouble concentrating, sleeping, and feelings of dejection and guilt. There are many types of depression. With ADHD, you might commonly see dysthymia, which consists of a depressed mood for many days, over- or undereating, sleeping too much or too little, low energy, low self-esteem, poor concentration, and feeling hopeless. Other forms of depression may also be present.

Learning Disabilities

Learning disabilities are problems with reading, writing, or mathematics. When given standardized tests, the student's ability or intelligence is substantially higher than his or her achievement is. Underachievement is generally considered age inappropriate. Children with ADHD frequently have problems with reading fluency and mathematical calculations. ADHD learning problems have to do with attention, memory, and executive function difficulties rather than with dyslexia, dysgraphia, or dyscalculia, which are learning disabilities. The point here is not to overlook either. Depending on how learning disabilities are defined, between 10 and 90 percent of youth with ADHD also have a learning disability (Robin, 1998).

Parent Options for Having Their Child Evaluated for ADHD

When a child is experiencing difficulties that suggest that he or she may have ADHD, parents/guardians can take one of two basic paths to evaluation. They can seek the services of an outside professional or clinic, or they can request that their local school district conduct an evaluation.

In pursuing a private evaluation or in selecting a professional to perform an assessment for ADHD, parents should consider the clinician's training and experience with the disorder, as well as his or her availability to coordinate the various treatment approaches. Most ADHD parent support groups know clinicians trained to evaluate and treat children with ADHD. Parents may also ask their child's pediatrician, a community mental health center, a university mental health clinic, or a hospital's child evaluation unit.

It is important for parents to realize, however, that the schools have an affirmative obligation to evaluate a child (aged three through twenty-one) if school personnel suspect that the child might have ADHD or any other disability that is adversely affecting educational performance. (That means the child must be having difficulties in school. Those difficulties include social, emotional, and behavioral problems, not just academic troubles.) This evaluation is provided free of charge to families and, by law, must involve more than one standardized test or procedure.

Thus if parents suspect that their child has an attention or hyperactivity problem, or if they know for certain that their child has ADHD and that their child's educational performance appears to be adversely affected, they should first request that the school system evaluate their child.

Evaluation When the Child Is a Toddler

If their child is under three years old and parents suspect that ADHD may be affecting their child's development, they may want to investigate what *early intervention services* are available in their state through the Part C program of the Individuals with Disabilities Education Act (IDEA).

Since ADHD is a developmental disorder, diagnosing young children requires some special consideration. For instance, toddlers do not pay attention for long periods, so a clinician would not necessarily find inattention in a toddler a symptom of ADHD. Also toddlers are more easily frustrated and do shift activities a lot. It is important that the person doing the diagnosis be very familiar with normal child development in order to determine what behaviors would be inappropriate for that age.

Parents can find out about the availability of early intervention services in their state by contacting the state agency responsible for administering early intervention services, by asking their pediatrician, or by contacting the nursery or child care department in their local hospital.

Preschoolers (children ages three through five) may be eligible for services under Part B of the IDEA. If the child is a preschooler, the parents may wish to contact the state Department of Education or local school district, ask a pediatrician, or talk with local day care providers about how to have the child assessed through the school district's special education department.

Also, under Head Start regulations, ADHD is considered a chronic or acute health impairment entitling the child to special education services when the child's inattention, hyperactivity, and impulsivity are developmentally inappropriate, chronic, and displayed in multiple settings and when the ADHD severely affects performance in normal developmental tasks (e.g., in planning and completing activities or following simple directions).

If their child is of school age (six or older), and the parents suspect that ADHD may be adversely affecting their child's educational performance, they can ask their local school district to conduct an evaluation. With the exception of the physical examination, the assessment can be conducted by school personnel as long as a member of the evaluation group is knowledgeable about assessing ADHD. If not, the district may need to use an outside professional consultant trained in ADHD assessment. This person must know what to look for during child observation; must be competent to conduct structured interviews with parents, teacher(s), and child; and must know how to administer and interpret behavior-rating scales.

However, if the school district does not believe that a child's educational performance is being adversely affected, it may refuse to evaluate the child. In this case, there are a number of actions parents can take including pursuing a private evaluation. It is also important to persist with the school, enlisting the assistance of an advocate if necessary. Parents can generally find this type of assistance by contacting the Parent Training and Information (PTI) center for their state, the Protection and Advocacy (P&A) agency, or a local parent group.

A school district's refusal to evaluate a child suspected of having ADHD involves issues that must be addressed on an individual basis. The parents' state's PTI center, P&A agency, or a local parent group will typically be able to provide information on a parent's legal rights, give specific suggestions on how to proceed, and in many cases, offer direct assistance. Parents may also use a special education attorney.

For children who are evaluated by the school system, eligibility for special education and related services will be based upon evaluation results and the specific policies of the state. Unfortunately, many parents have found this to be a problematic area as well.

Conclusion

Not everyone who is overly hyperactive, inattentive, or impulsive has ADHD. Since most people sometimes blurt out things they did not mean to say, jump from one task to another, or become disorganized and forgetful, how can specialists tell if the problem is ADHD? Because everyone shows some of these behaviors at times, the diagnosis requires that such behavior be demonstrated to a degree that is inappropriate for the person's age. The diagnostic guidelines also contain specific requirements for determining when the symptoms indicate ADHD. The behaviors must appear early in life, before age seven, must and continue for at least six months. Above all, the behaviors must create a real handicap in at least two areas of a person's life such as in the schoolroom, on the playground, at home, in the community, or in social settings. So someone who shows some symptoms but whose schoolwork or friendships are not impaired by these behaviors would not be diagnosed with ADHD. Nor would a child who seems overly active on the playground but functions well elsewhere receive an ADHD diagnosis.

To assess whether a child has ADHD, specialists consider several critical questions: Are these behaviors excessive, long term, and pervasive? That is, do they occur more often than in other children the same age? Are they a continuous problem, not just a response to a temporary situation? Do the behaviors occur in several settings or only in one specific place like the playground or in the schoolroom? The person's pattern of behavior is compared against a set of criteria and characteristics of the disorder as listed in the *DSM-IV-TR*.

Step VI

Identifying Treatment Options for Students With ADHD

Like many medical conditions, ADHD is managed, not cured. There is no "quick fix" that resolves the symptoms of the disorder. Yet a lot can be done to help. Through effective management, some of the secondary problems that often arise out of untreated ADHD may be avoided. In the majority of cases, ADHD management will be a life-long endeavor. It may be helpful to think of ADHD as a challenge that can be met. The National Institute of Mental Health (NIMH), in combination with the U.S. Department of Education's Office of Special Education Programs (OSEP), completed a long-term, multi-site study to determine which treatments had the greatest positive effect on reducing ADHD symptoms. This study is known as the MTA study (MTA Cooperative Group, 1999a). MTA stands for multimodal treatment study of children with ADHD.

Although at present, no cure for ADHD exists, a number of treatment options have proven to be effective for some children. Effective strategies include behavioral, pharmacological, and multimodal methods.

What is the recommended multimodal treatment for ADHD? The recommended multimodal treatment approach consists of four core interventions:

1. patient, parent, and teacher education about the disorder;

2. medication (usually from the class of drugs called stimulants);

3. behavioral therapy; and

4. other environmental supports, including an appropriate school program.

Each of these core interventions is described in more detail in the following sections.

Parent, Child, and Teacher Education

Often, the first treatment step begins with learning what ADHD is and what to do about it. This knowledge will help parents understand that the way their child thinks, acts, and feels has a lot to do with circumstances outside his or her control. When we understand the nature of the challenge, we are better equipped to meet the challenge.

Understanding ADHD also changes the way in which a child's behavior is viewed. When we know more about ADHD, we come to understand that *the child has troubles and is not the cause of those troubles.*

There are accommodations that can help parents' sons or daughters adapt reasonably well. It is critical for parents to learn what these accommodations are and to work to see that they are put in place across different environments—school, home, and community. Children with ADHD need strong advocates. They also need to be taught self-advocacy skills if they are to successfully manage their symptoms throughout life. Self-advocacy should begin early in life. Parents need to help their children understand and identify their difficulties. Teaching them how to ask for help and accommodations is an essential part of attaining success.

Medication

The MTA study found medication to be very effective in the management of ADHD symptoms. However, pharmacological treatment remains one of the most common, yet most controversial, forms of ADHD treatment. It is important to note that the decision to prescribe any medicine is the responsibility of medical—not educational—professionals, after consultation with the family and agreement on the most appropriate treatment plan. Pharmacological treatment includes the use of psychostimulants, antidepressants, antianxiety medications, antipsychotics, and mood stabilizers (NIMH, 2000).

Stimulants predominate in clinical use and have been found to be effective with 75 to 90 percent of children with ADHD (U.S. Department of Health and Human Services [DHHS], 1999). Stimulants include Methylphenidate (Ritalin), Dextroamphetamine (Dexedrine), and Pemoline (Cylert). Other types of medication (antidepressants, antianxiety medications, antipsychotics, and mood stabilizers) are used primarily for those who do not respond to stimulants, or those who have coexisting disorders. The results of the MTA study, which are discussed in further detail in the next section, confirm research findings on the use of pharmacological treatment for patients with ADHD. Specifically, the study found that the use of medication was almost as effective as the multimodal treatment of medication and behavioral interventions (Edwards, 2002).

Administering Medication at School

Researchers believe that psychostimulants affect the portion of the brain that is responsible for producing neurotransmitters. Neurotransmitters are chemical agents at nerve endings that help electrical impulses travel among nerve cells. Neurotransmitters are responsible for helping people attend to important aspects of their environment. The appropriate medication stimulates these under-functioning chemicals to produce extra neurotransmitters, thus increasing the child's capacity to pay attention, control impulses, and reduce hyperactivity. Medication necessary to achieve this typically requires multiple doses throughout the day, as an individual dose of the medication lasts for a short time (one to four hours). However, slow- or timed-release forms of the medication (e.g., Concerta) may allow a child with ADHD to continue to benefit from medication over a longer period. Doctors, teachers, and parents should communicate openly about the child's behavior and disposition in order to get the dosage and schedule to a point where the child can perform optimally in both academic and social settings while keeping side effects to a minimum. However, it is recommended that medication be taken before or after school if it is determined that the child should receive medication during the school day. It is important to develop a plan to ensure that medication is administered in accordance with the plan. Such a plan would be an appropriate component of the child's IEP. In addition, schools must ensure that the child's and parent's rights to medical confidentiality are maintained.

The American Academy of Pediatrics (AAP) found that at least 80 percent of children will respond to one of the stimulants if they are administered in a systematic way. Under medical care, children who fail to show positive effects or who experience intolerable side effects on one type of medication may find another medication helpful. The AAP (2001) reported that children who do not respond to one medication may have a positive response to an alternative medication, and concludes that stimulants may be a safe and effective way to treat ADHD in children.

In January 2003, a new type of nonstimulant medication for the treatment of children and adults with ADHD was approved by the U.S. Food and Drug Adminstration (FDA). Atomoxetine, also known as Straterra, may be prescribed by physicians in some cases. The medications that seem to be the most effective are a class of drugs known as stimulants.

The FDA recently approved a medication for ADHD that is not a stimulant. The medication Strattera, or atomoxetine, works on the neurotransmitter norepinephrine, whereas the stimulants primarily work on dopamine. Both of theses neurotransmitters are believed to play a role in ADHD. More studies must be done to contrast Strattera with the medications already available, but the evidence to date indicates that over 70 percent of children with ADHD who are given Strattera manifest significant improvement in their symptoms.

Some people get better results from one medication, some from another. It is important to work with the prescribing physician to find the right medication and the right dosage. For many people, the stimulants dramatically reduce their hyperactivity and impulsivity and improve their ability to focus, work, and learn. The medications may also improve physical coordination such as that needed in handwriting and in sports.

The stimulant drugs, when used with medical supervision, are usually considered quite safe. Stimulants do not make the child feel "high," although some children say they feel different or funny. Such changes are usually very minor. Although some parents worry that their child may become addicted to the medication, to date there is no convincing evidence that stimulant medications, when used for treatment of ADHD, cause drug abuse or dependence. A review of all long-term studies on stimulant medication and substance abuse, conducted by researchers at Massachusetts General Hospital and Harvard Medical School, found that teenagers with ADHD who remained on their medication during the teen years had a lower likelihood of substance use or abuse than did ADHD adolescents who were not taking medications (U.S. Department of Education, 2004).

The stimulant drugs come in long- and short-term forms. The newer, sustained-release stimulants can be taken before school and are long lasting so that the child does not need to go to the school nurse every day for a pill. The doctor can discuss with the parents the child's needs and decide which preparation to use and whether the child needs to take the medicine during school hours only or in the evening and on weekends too.

If the child does not show symptoms of improvement after taking a particular medication for a specified time, the doctor may try adjusting the dosage. If there is still no improvement, the child may be switched to another medication. About one out of ten children is not helped by a stimulant medication. Other types of medication may be used if stimulants do not work or if the ADHD occurs with another disorder. Antidepressants and other medications can help control symptoms accompanying depression or anxiety.

Sometimes the doctor may prescribe for a young child a medication that has been approved by the FDA for use in adults or older children. This use of the medication is called *off label*. Many of the newer medications that are proving helpful for child mental disorders are prescribed off label because only a few of them have been systematically studied for safety and efficacy in children. Medications that have not undergone such testing are dispensed with the statement that "safety and efficacy have not been established in pediatric patients."

The decision to place a child on medication may not be an easy one, especially given the controversy that surrounds the stimulants, specifically Ritalin. There have been many reports that medication is overprescribed for treatment of ADHD. However, according to the American Medical Association's (AMA) Council on Scientific Affairs (Goldman, Genel, Bezman, & Slanetz, 1998), "There is no widespread overprescription of methylphenidate by physicians" (p. 1100). By following good diagnostic procedures, the chances of overprescribing this medication are significantly reduced. Some children cannot take stimulant medications. In these cases, the physician knows what other medications can be helpful in relieving ADHD symptoms. Medication may not be the right approach for every child.

Side Effects of ADHD Medications

Most side effects of the stimulant medications are minor and are usually related to the dosage of the medication being taken. Higher doses produce more side effects. The most common side effects are decreased appetite, insomnia, increased anxiety, tics, and/or irritability. Some children report mild stomachaches or headaches.

Appetite seems to fluctuate, usually being low during the middle of the day and more normal by suppertime. Adequate amounts of nutritional food should be available for the child, especially at peak appetite times.

If the child has difficulty falling asleep, several options may be tried: a lower dosage of the stimulant, giving the stimulant earlier in the day, discontinuing the afternoon or evening dosage, or giving an adjunct medication such as a low-dosage antidepressant or clonidine. A few children develop tics during treatment. These can often be lessened by changing the medication dosage. A very few children cannot tolerate any stimulant, no matter how low the dosage. In such cases, the child is often given an antidepressant instead of the stimulant.

When a child's schoolwork and behavior improve soon after starting medication, the child, parents, and teachers tend to applaud the drug for causing the sudden changes. Unfortunately, when people see such immediate improvement, they often think medication is all that is needed. But medications do not cure ADHD; they only control the symptoms on the day they are taken. Although the medications help the child pay better attention and complete schoolwork, they cannot increase knowledge or improve academic skills. The medications help the child to use those skills he or she already possesses.

Finally, some parents are reluctant to place their child on medication for fear that doing so may lead to later substance abuse. Researchers have looked into this concern quite seriously. Research supports previous findings that stimulant medication treatment may actually prevent later substance abuse (Zametkin & Ernst, 1999). As with any medication, though, parents must carefully monitor its use to be sure that the medication is taken as prescribed.

Final Points About Medication for ADHD

Since ADHD appears to be primarily a neurobiochemically based problem, it stands to reason that medication that gets to the core of the problem would be effective. The medication most often used is stimulant medication, especially methylphenidate. Most people know this medication as the drug Ritalin. There are other stimulant medications—Concerta, Metadate, Dexedrine, Cylert, and Adderall, an amphetamine compound.

These medications are believed to work by stimulating the action of the brain's neurotransmitters, especially dopamine. With the brain's systems working more efficiently, attention, memory, and executive functions including inhibition are improved. The result is better concentration, increased working memory capacity, greater recall, less hyperactivity, and more impulse control. Stimulant medications do not tend to help with symptoms of anxiety or depression (Barkley, DuPaul, & O'Connor, 1999).

Parents should always discuss any medication treatment thoroughly with their child's physician. He or she should explain the benefits and the drawbacks of medication to them and to their child if appropriate. When medication is first prescribed, the physician should start with a low dose and then gradually raise it until the symptoms improve. Parents will need to dispense the medication as prescribed and closely monitor its effects including any side effects. With stimulants, most side effects are quite mild and go away over time. Since a child spends a large portion of his or her day at school, parents will also need to be in contact with their child's teachers to determine positive effects and side effects. Communicate with the physician often, especially when medication is started. Parents should call immediately with any problems or questions.

Also be aware that especially during adolescence many teens actively resist taking medication. If this happens, it is wise for parents to discuss the situation with the child's doctor. While medication cannot be forced on an unwilling patient, the doctor may have some ideas of how to work with the teenager about any resistance to taking the medication.

The bottom line with medication is

- medications for ADHD help many children focus and be more successful at school, home, and play; and
- about 80 percent of children who need medication for ADHD still need it as teenagers; over 50 percent need medication as adults.

Behavioral Therapy

As parents and teachers know, ADHD can cause significant inappropriate behavior. Frequent complaints include failure to follow rules, listen to commands, complete tasks, delay gratification, or control impulse. In addition, some youth may be aggressive or anxious.

These symptoms lead to their own set of problems such as avoiding tasks or fighting. It is very easy for everyone involved—the child, the parents, and the teacher(s)—to be worn down into a pattern of negative and sometimes hostile interactions. This cycle, however, can be broken, and different, more positive interactions and behavior patterns can be developed. Knowing more about behavior and how to support behavior that is positive and appropriate is extremely useful information for any parent or teacher of a child with ADHD.

Behavioral approaches represent a broad set of specific interventions that have the common goal of modifying the physical and social environment to alter or change behavior (AAP, 2001). They are used in the treatment of ADHD to provide structure for the child and to reinforce appropriate behavior. Those who typically implement behavioral approaches include parents as well as a wide range of professionals such as psychologists, school personnel, community mental health therapists, and primary care physicians. Types of behavioral approaches include behavioral training for parents and teachers (in which the parent and/or teacher is taught child management skills), a systematic program of contingency management (e.g., positive reinforcement, "time outs," response cost, and token economy), clinical behavioral therapy (training in problem solving and social skills), and cognitive-behavioral treatment (e.g., self-monitoring, verbal self-instruction, development of problem-solving strategies, self-reinforcement; AAP, 2001; Barkley, 1998b; Pelham, Wheeler, & Chronis, 1998). In general, these approaches are designed to use direct teaching and reinforcement strategies for positive behaviors and direct consequences for inappropriate behavior. Of these options, systematic programs of intensive contingency management conducted in specialized classrooms and summer camps with the setting controlled by highly trained individuals have been found to be highly effective (Abramowitz, Eckstrand, O'Leary, & Dulcan, 1992; Carlson, Pelham, Milich, & Dixon, 1992; Pelham & Hoza, 1996). A later study conducted by Pelham et al. (1998) indicates that two approaches—parent training in behavior therapy and classroom behavior interventions—also are successful in changing the behavior of children with ADHD. In addition, home-school interactions that support a consistent approach are important to the success of behavioral approaches.

The use of behavioral strategies holds promise but also presents some limitations. Behavioral strategies may be appealing to parents and professionals for the following reasons:

- Behavioral strategies are used most commonly when parents do not want to give their child medication.
- Behavioral strategies also can be used in conjunction with medicine (see multimodal methods).
- Behavioral techniques can be applied in a variety of settings including school, home, and the community.
- Behavioral strategies may be the only options if the child has an adverse reaction to medication.

The research results on the effectiveness of behavioral techniques are mixed. While studies that compare the behavior of children during periods on and off behavior therapy demonstrate the effectiveness of behavior therapy (Pelham & Fabiano, 2001), it is difficult to isolate its effectiveness. The multiplicity of interventions and outcome measures makes careful analysis of the effects of behavior therapy alone, or in association with medications, very difficult (AAP, 2001). A review conducted by McInerney, Reeve, and Kane (1995) confirms that the effective education of children with ADHD requires modifications to academic instruction, behavior management, and classroom environment. Although some research suggests that behavioral methods offer the opportunity for children to work on their strengths and learn self-management, other research indicates that behavioral interventions are effective but to a lower degree than treatment with psychostimulants (Jadad, Boyle, & Cunningham, 1999; Pelham et al., 1998).

Behavior therapy has been found to be effective only when it is implemented and maintained (AAP, 2001). Indeed, behavioral strategies can be difficult to implement consistently across all of the settings necessary for it to be maximally effective. Although behavioral management programs have been shown to enhance the academic performance and behavior of children with ADHD, follow-up and maintenance of the treatment is often lacking (Rapport, Stoner, & Jones, 1986).

In fact, some research has shown that behavioral techniques may fail to reduce ADHD's core characteristics of hyperactivity, impulsivity, and inattention (AAP, 2001; DHHS, 1999). Conversely, one must consider that the problems of children with ADHD are seldom limited to the core symptoms themselves (Barkley, 1990a). Children frequently demonstrate other types of psychosocial difficulties such as aggression, oppositional defiant behavior, academic underachievement, and depression (Barkley, 1990a). Because many of these other difficulties cannot be managed through psychostimulants, behavioral interventions may be useful in addressing ADHD and other problems a child may be exhibiting. (Specific behavioral interventions will be discussed in Step 9 of this book.)

Educational Interventions

One of the most critical areas in which to offer support is in the school arena. This is where most children with ADHD experience the greatest difficulty. That is because schools require great skill in the areas where students with ADHD are the weakest: attention, executive function, and memory. Although ADHD does not interfere with the ability to learn, it does wreak havoc on performance. Behavior problems, which usually get the most attention, may actually be by-products of the school environment and ADHD. These usually occur when tasks are too long, or too hard, or when tasks lack interest. Many behavior problems can be avoided or lessened by adapting the school setting to fit the needs of the student.

In the school arena, ADHD is an *educational performance problem*. When little or nothing is done to help children with ADHD improve their performance, over time they will show academic achievement problems. This underachievement is not the result of an inability to learn. It is caused by the cumulative effects of missing important blocks of information and skill development that build from lesson to lesson and from one school year to the next.

Generally, ADHD will affect the student in one or more of the following performance areas:

- starting tasks;
- staying on task;
- completing tasks;
- making transitions;
- interacting with others;
- following through on directions;
- producing work at consistently normal levels; and/or
- organizing multistep tasks.

Those teaching or designing programs for students with ADHD need to pinpoint where each student's difficulties occur. Otherwise, valuable intervention resources may be spent in areas where they are not critical.

For example, one child with ADHD may have difficulty starting a task because the directions are not clear. Another student may fully understand the directions but many forget to follow all of them. Another may have difficulty making transitions and, as a result, get stuck in the space where one task ends and another begins. With the first child, intervention needs to focus upon making directions clear and in helping the child to understand those directions. The second child would need guidance to follow all the directions. The third child would need help in making transitions from one activity to another.

The sooner educational interventions begin, the better. They should be started when educational performance problems become evident and should not be delayed because the child is still holding his or her own on achievement tests. (Specific educational interventions will be discussed later in this book.)

Conclusion

Research indicates that for many children the best way to mitigate symptoms of ADHD is the use of a combined approach. A recent study by the NIMH—the MTA study—is the longest and most thorough study of the effects of ADHD interventions (MTA Cooperative Group, 1999a, 1999b). The study followed 579 children between the ages of seven and ten at six sites nationwide and in Canada. The researchers compared the effects of four interventions: (a) medication provided by the researchers, (b) behavioral intervention, a combination of medication and behavioral intervention, and (c) no-intervention community care (i.e., typical medical care provided in the community).

Multimodal intervention improves

- academic performance,
- parent-child interaction, and
- school-related behavior;

and reduces

- child anxiety and
- oppositional behavior.

Of the four interventions investigated, the researchers found that the combined medication/behavior treatment and the medication treatment work significantly better than behavioral therapy alone or community care alone at reducing the symptoms of ADHD. Multimodal treatments were especially effective in improving social skills for students coming from high-stress environments and children with ADHD in combination with symptoms of anxiety or depression. The study revealed that a lower medication dosage is effective in multimodal treatments, whereas higher doses were needed to achieve similar results in the medication-only treatment.

Researchers found improvement in the following areas after using a multimodal intervention: child anxiety, academic performance, oppositional behavior, and parent-child interaction. Positive results also were found in school-related behavior when multimodal treatment is coupled with improved parenting skills including more effective disciplinary responses and appropriate reinforcements (Hinshaw et al., 2000). These findings were replicated across all six research sites, despite substantial differences among sites in their samples' sociodemographic characteristics. The study's overall results appear to apply to a wide range of children and families identified as in need of treatment services for ADHD (NIMH, 2000). Other studies demonstrate that multimodal treatments hold value for those children for whom treatment with medication alone is not sufficient (Klein et al., 1997).

In October of 2001, the AAP released evidence-based recommendations for the treatment of children diagnosed with ADHD. Their guidelines state that

- primary care clinicians should establish a treatment program that recognizes ADHD as a chronic condition;
- the treating clinician, parents, and the child, in collaboration with school personnel, should specify appropriate target outcomes to guide management;
- the clinician should recommend stimulant mediation and/or behavioral therapy as appropriate to improve target outcomes in children with ADHD;
- when the selected management for a child with ADHD has not met target outcomes, clinicians should evaluate the original diagnosis, the use of all appropriate treatments, the adherence to the treatment plan, and the presence of coexisting conditions; and
- the clinician should periodically provide a systematic follow-up for the child with ADHD. Monitoring should be directed to target outcomes and adverse effects, with information gathered from parents, teachers, and the child.

The AAP (2001) report stressed that the treatment of ADHD (whether behavioral, pharmacological, or multimodal) requires the development of child-specific treatment plans that describe not only the methods and goals of treatment, but also include means of monitoring over time and specific plans for follow-up. The process of developing target outcomes requires careful input from parents, children, and teachers as well as other school personnel where available and appropriate. The AAP concluded that parents, children, and educators should agree on at least three to six key targets and desired changes as requisites for constructing the treatment plan. The goals should be realistic, attainable, and measurable. The AAP report found that, for most children, stimulant medication is highly effective in the management of the core symptoms of ADHD. For many children, behavioral interventions are valuable as primary treatment or as an adjunct in the management of ADHD, based on the nature of coexisting conditions, specific target outcomes, and family circumstances (AAP, 2001).

Step VII

Understanding the Key Components to Effective Classroom Management for Students With ADHD

Teachers who are often successful in educating children with ADHD use a three-pronged strategy. They begin by identifying the unique needs of the child. For example, the teacher determines how, when, and why the child is inattentive, impulsive, and hyperactive. The teacher then selects different educational practices associated with academic instruction, behavioral interventions, and classroom accommodations that are appropriate to meet that child's needs. Finally, the teacher combines these practices into an individualized educational program (IEP) or other individualized plan and integrates this program with educational activities provided to other children in the class. The three-pronged strategy, in summary, is as follows.

1. Evaluate the Child's Individual Needs and Strengths

Assess the unique educational needs and strengths of a child with ADHD in the class. Working with a multidisciplinary team and the child's parents/guardians, consider both academic and behavioral needs, using formal diagnostic assessments and informal classroom observations. Assessments such as learning style inventories can be used to determine children's strengths and enable instruction to build on their existing abilities. The settings and contexts in which challenging behaviors occur should be considered in the evaluation.

2. Select Appropriate Instructional Practices

Determine which instructional practices will meet the academic and behavioral needs identified for the child. Select practices that fit the content, are age appropriate, and gain the attention of the child.

3. For Children Receiving Special Education Services, Integrate Appropriate Practices Within an IEP

In consultation with other educators and parents, an IEP should be created to reflect annual goals and the special-education-related services, along with supplementary aids and services necessary for attaining those goals. Plan how to integrate the educational activities provided to other children in your class with those selected for the child with ADHD.

Because no two children with ADHD are alike, it is important to keep in mind that no single educational program, practice, or setting will be best for all children.

Components of Successful Classroom Management for Children With ADHD

Successful programs for children with ADHD integrate the following three components:

1. academic instruction;
2. behavioral interventions; and
3. classroom accommodations.

The remainder of this book describes how to integrate a program using these three components and provides suggestions for practices that can help children with ADHD in a classroom setting. It should be emphasized that many of the techniques suggested have the additional benefit of enhancing the learning of other children in the classroom who *do not* have ADHD.

Step VIII

Implementing Academic Instruction Techniques

The first major component of the most effective instruction for children with ADHD is effective academic instruction. Teachers can help prepare their students with ADHD to achieve by applying the principles of effective teaching when they introduce, conduct, and conclude each lesson. The discussion and techniques that follow pertain to the instructional process in general (across subject areas); strategies for specific subject areas appear in the subsequent subsection "Individualizing Instructional Practices."

Introducing Lessons

Students with ADHD learn best with a carefully structured academic lesson—one where the teacher explains what he or she wants children to learn in the current lesson and places these skills and knowledge in the context of previous lessons. Effective teachers preview their expectations about what students will learn and how they should behave during the lesson. A number of teaching-related practices have been found especially useful in facilitating this process:

- **Provide an advance organizer.** Prepare students for the day's lesson by quickly summarizing the order of various activities planned. Explain, for example, that a review of the previous lesson will be followed by new information and that both group and independent work will be expected.

- **Set learning expectations.** State what students are expected to learn during the lesson. For example, explain to students that a language arts lesson will involve reading a story about Paul Bunyan and identifying new vocabulary words in the story.

- **Review previous lessons.** Review information about previous lessons on this topic. For example, remind children that yesterday's lesson focused on learning how to regroup in subtraction. Review several problems before describing the current lesson.

- **Set behavioral expectations.** Describe how students are expected to behave during the lesson. For example, tell children that they may talk quietly to their neighbors as they do their seatwork or they may raise their hands to get your attention.

- **State needed materials.** Identify all materials that the children will need during the lesson, rather than leaving them to figure out on their own the materials required. For example, specify that children need their journals and pencils for journal writing or their crayons, scissors, and colored paper for an art project.

- **Explain additional resources.** Tell students how to obtain help in mastering the lesson. For example, refer children to a particular page in the textbook for guidance on completing a worksheet.

- **Simplify instructions, choices, and scheduling.** The simpler the expectations communicated to an ADHD student, the more likely it is that he or she will comprehend and complete them in a timely and productive manner.

Conducting Lessons

In order to conduct the most productive lessons for children with ADHD, effective teachers periodically question children's understanding of the material, probe for correct answers before calling on other students, and identify which students need additional assistance. Teachers should keep in mind that transitions from one lesson or class to another are particularly difficult for students with ADHD. When they are prepared for transitions, these children are more likely to respond and to stay on task. The following set of strategies may assist teachers in conducting effective lessons:

- **Be predictable.** Structure and consistency are very important for children with ADHD; many do not deal well with change. Minimal rules and minimal choices are best. They need to understand clearly what is expected of them, as well as the consequences for not adhering to expectations.

- **Support the student's participation in the classroom.** Provide students with ADHD with private, discreet cues to stay on task and advance warning that they will be called upon shortly. Avoid bringing attention to differences between ADHD students and their classmates. At all times, avoid the use of sarcasm and criticism.

- **Use computer technology.** Use a variety of computer technology tools to present academic lessons. For example, use the computer to demonstrate how to solve an addition problem requiring regrouping. The students can work on the problem at their desks while you manipulate counters on an enhanced computer screen.

- **Check student performance.** Question individual students to assess their mastery of the lesson. For example, you can ask students doing seatwork (i.e., lessons completed by students at their desks in the classroom) to demonstrate how they arrived at the answer to a problem, or you can ask individual students to state, in their own words, how the main character felt at the end of the story.

- **Ask probing questions.** Probe for the correct answer after allowing a child sufficient time to work out the answer to a question. Count at least fifteen seconds before giving the answer or calling on another student. Ask follow-up questions that give children an opportunity to demonstrate what they know.

- **Perform ongoing student evaluation.** Identify students who need additional assistance. Watch for signs of lack of comprehension such as daydreaming or visual or verbal indications of frustration. Provide these children with extra explanations, or ask another student to serve as a peer tutor for the lesson.

- **Help students correct their own mistakes.** Describe how students can identify and correct their own mistakes. For example, remind students that they should check their calculations in math problems and reiterate how they can check their calculations; remind students of particularly difficult spelling rules and how students can watch out for easy-to-make errors.

- Remind students to keep working and to focus on their assigned task. For example, you can provide follow-up directions or assign learning partners. These practices can be directed at individual children or at the entire class.
- **Follow-up directions.** Effective teachers of children with ADHD also guide them with follow-up directions:
  - *Oral directions.* After giving directions to the class as a whole, provide additional oral directions for a student with ADHD. For example, ask the child if he or she understood the directions and repeat the directions together.
  - *Written directions.* Provide follow-up directions in writing. For example, write the page number for an assignment on the chalkboard and remind the child to look at the chalkboard if he or she forgets the assignment.
- **Lower noise level.** Monitor the noise level in the classroom, and provide corrective feedback as needed. If the noise level exceeds the level appropriate for the type of lesson, remind all students—or individual students—about the behavioral rules stated at the beginning of the lesson. Remember, the softer you speak, the quieter they become.
- **Divide work into smaller units.** Break down assignments into smaller, less complex tasks. For example, allow students to complete five math problems before presenting them with the remaining five problems.
- **Highlight key points.** Highlight key words in the instructions on worksheets to help the child with ADHD focus on the directions. Prepare the worksheet before the lesson begins, or underline or highlight in yellow key words as you and the child read the directions together. When reading, show children how to identify and highlight a key sentence, or have them write it on a separate piece of paper, before asking for a summary of the entire book. In math, show children how to underline the important facts and operations; in "Mary has two apples, and John has three," underline "two," "and," and "three."
- **Eliminate or reduce frequency of timed tests.** Tests that are timed may not allow children with ADHD to demonstrate what they truly know due to their potential preoccupation with elapsed time. Allow students with ADHD more time to

complete quizzes and tests in order to eliminate "test anxiety," and provide them with other opportunities, methods, or test formats to demonstrate their knowledge.

- **Use cooperative learning strategies.** Have students work together in small groups to maximize their own and each other's learning (Slavin, 2002).
- **Use assistive technology.** All students and those with ADHD in particular can benefit from the use of technology (e.g., PDAs and projector screens), which makes instruction more visual and allows students to participate actively.

Concluding Lessons

Effective teachers conclude their lessons by providing advance warning that the lesson is about to end, checking the completed assignments of at least some of the students with ADHD, and instructing students how to begin preparing for the next activity.

- **Provide advance warnings.** Provide advance warning that a lesson is about to end. Announce five or ten minutes before the end of the lesson (particularly for seatwork and group projects) how much time remains. You may also want to tell students at the beginning of the lesson how much time they will have to complete it.
- **Check assignments.** Check completed assignments for at least some students. Review what they have learned during the lesson to get a sense of how ready the class was for the lesson and how to plan the next lesson.
- **Preview the next lesson.** Instruct students on how to begin preparing for the next lesson. For example, inform children that they need to put away their textbooks and come to the front of the room for a large group spelling lesson.

Individualizing Instructional Practices

In addition to the general strategies listed previously for introducing, conducting, and concluding their lessons, effective teachers of students with ADHD also individualize their instructional practices in accordance with different academic subjects and the needs of their students within each area. This is because children with ADHD have different ways of learning and retaining information, not all of which involve traditional reading and listening. Effective teachers first identify areas in which each child requires extra assistance, and then they use special strategies to provide structured opportunities for the child to review and master an academic lesson that was previously presented to the entire class. Strategies that may help facilitate this goal include the following (grouped by subject area).

Language Arts and Reading Comprehension

To help children with ADHD who are poor readers improve their reading comprehension skills, try the following instructional practices:

- **Silent reading time.** Establish a fixed time each day for silent reading (e.g., D.E.A.R.: drop everything and read; and S.S.R.: sustained silent reading; Holt & O'Tuel, 1989; Manzo & Zehr, 1998).
- **Follow-along reading.** Ask the child to read a story silently while listening to other students or the teacher read the story aloud to the entire class.
- **Partner reading activities.** Pair the child with ADHD with another student partner who is a strong reader. The partners take turns reading orally and listening to each other.
- **Storyboards.** Ask the child to make storyboards that illustrate the sequence of main events in a story.
- **Storytelling.** Schedule storytelling sessions where the child can retell a story that he or she has read recently.
- **Playacting.** Schedule playacting sessions where the child can role-play different characters in a favorite story.
- **Word bank.** Keep a word bank or dictionary of new or "hard-to-read" sight-vocabulary words.
- **Board games for reading comprehension.** Play board games that provide practice with target reading-comprehension skills or sight-vocabulary words.
- **Computer games for reading comprehension.** Schedule computer time for the child to have drill and practice with sight vocabulary words.
- **Recorded books.** These materials, available from many libraries, can stimulate interest in traditional reading and can be used to reinforce and complement reading lessons.
- **"Backup" materials for home use.** Make available to students a second set of books and materials that they can use at home.

- **Summary materials.** Allow and encourage students to use published book summaries, synopses, and digests of major reading assignments to review (not replace) reading assignments.

Phonics

To help children with ADHD master rules of phonics, the following are effective:

- **Mnemonics for phonics.** Teach the child mnemonics that provide reminders about hard-to-learn phonics rules (e.g., "when two vowels go walking, the first does the talking"; Scruggs & Mastropieri, 2000).
- **Word families.** Teach the child to recognize and read word families that illustrate particular phonetic concepts (e.g., "ph" sounds, "at-bat-cat").
- **Board games for phonics.** Have students play board games such as bingo that allow them to practice phonetically irregular words.
- **Computer games for phonics.** Use a computer to provide opportunities for students to drill and practice with phonics or grammar lessons.
- **Picture-letter charts.** Use these for children who know sounds but do not know the letters that go with them.

Writing

In composing stories or other writing assignments, children with ADHD benefit from the following practices:

- **Standards for writing assignments.** Identify and teach the child classroom standards for acceptable written work such as format and style.
- **Recognizing parts of a story.** Teach the student how to describe the major parts of a story (e.g., plot, main characters, setting, conflict, and resolution). Use a storyboard with parts listed for this purpose.
- **Post office.** Establish a post office in the classroom, and provide students with opportunities to write, mail, and receive letters to and from their classmates and teacher.
- **Visualize compositions.** Ask the child to close his or her eyes and visualize a paragraph that the teacher reads aloud. Another variation of this technique is to ask a student to

describe a recent event while the other students close their eyes and visualize what is being said as a written paragraph.

- **Proofread compositions.** Require that the child proofread his or her work before turning in written assignments. Provide the child with a list of items to check when proofreading his or her own work.

- **Computers.** Ask the student to dictate writing assignments using a computer program, as an alternative to writing them.

- **Dictate writing assignments.** Have the teacher or another student write down a story told by a child with ADHD.

Spelling

To help children with ADHD who are poor spellers, the following techniques have been found to be helpful:

- **Everyday examples of hard-to-spell words.** Take advantage of everyday events to teach difficult spelling words in context. For example, ask a child eating a cheese sandwich to spell "sandwich."

- **Frequently used words.** Assign spelling words that the child routinely uses in his or her speech each day.

- **Dictionary of misspelled words.** Ask the child to keep a personal dictionary of frequently misspelled words.

- **Partner spelling activities.** Pair the child with another student. Ask the partners to quiz each other on the spelling of new words. Encourage both students to guess the correct spelling.

- **Manipulatives.** Use cutout letters or other manipulatives to spell out hard-to-learn words.

- **Color-coded letters.** Color code different letters in hard-to-spell words (e.g., "receipt").

- **Movement activities.** Combine movement activities with spelling lessons (e.g., jump rope while spelling words out loud).

- **Word banks.** Use three-inch by five-inch index cards of frequently misspelled words sorted alphabetically.

Handwriting

Students with ADHD who have difficulty with manuscript or cursive writing may well benefit from their teacher's use of the following instructional practices:

- **Individual wipe boards.** Ask the child to practice copying and erasing the target words on a small, individual wipe board. Two children can be paired to practice their target words together.
- **Quiet places for handwriting.** Provide the child with a special "quiet place" (e.g., a table outside the classroom) to complete his or her handwriting assignments.
- **Spacing words on a page.** Teach the child to use his or her finger to measure how much space to leave between each word in a written assignment.
- **Special writing paper.** Ask the child to use special paper with vertical lines to learn to space letters and words on a page.
- **Structured programs for handwriting.** Teach handwriting skills through a structured program such as Jan Olsen's (2003) *Handwriting Without Tears* program.

Math Computation

Numerous individualized instructional practices can help children with ADHD improve their basic computation skills. The following are just a few:

- **Patterns in math.** Teach the student to recognize patterns when adding, subtracting, multiplying, or dividing whole numbers (e.g., the digits of numbers that are multiples of 9—18, 27, 36—add up to 9).
- **Partnering for math activities.** Pair a child with ADHD with another student and provide opportunities for the partners to quiz each other about basic computation skills.
- **Mastery of math symbols.** If children do not understand the symbols used in math, they will not be able to do the work. For instance, do they understand that the "plus" in 1 + 3 means to add and that the "minus" in 5 − 3 means to take away?
- **Mnemonics for basic computation.** Teach the child mnemonics that describe basic steps in computing whole numbers. For example, "Don't Miss Susie's Boat" can be used to help the student recall the basic steps in long division (i.e., divide, multiply, subtract, and bring down).
- **Real-life examples of money skills.** Provide the child with real-life opportunities to practice target money skills. For example, ask the child to calculate his or her change when

paying for lunch in the school cafeteria, or set up a class store where children can practice calculating change.

- **Color coding arithmetic symbols.** Color code basic arithmetic symbols such as +, −, and = to provide visual cues for children when they are computing whole numbers.
- **Calculators to check basic computation.** Ask the child to use a calculator to check addition, subtraction, multiplication, or division.
- **Board games for basic computation.** Ask the child to play board games to practice adding, subtracting, multiplying, and dividing whole numbers.
- **Computer games for basic computation.** Schedule computer time for the child to drill and practice basic computations, using appropriate games.
- **"Magic minute" drills.** Have students perform a quick (sixty-second) drill every day to practice basic computation of math facts, and have children track their own performance. However, be careful, beacsue you want to be sure that the time frame for a "speed drill" is always one in which the child can succeed.

Solving Math Word Problems

To help children with ADHD improve their skill in solving word problems in mathematics, try the following:

- **Reread the problem.** Teach the child to read a word problem *two times* before beginning to compute the answer.
- **Clue words.** Teach the child clue words that identify which operation to use when solving word problems. For example, words such as "sum," "total," or "all together" may indicate an addition operation.
- **Guiding questions for word problems.** Teach students to ask guiding questions in solving word problems. For example, what is the question asked in the problem? What information do you need to figure out the answer? What operation should you use to compute the answer?
- **Real-life examples of word problems.** Ask the student to create and solve word problems that provide practice with specific target operations, such as addition, subtraction, multiplication, or division. These problems can be based on recent, real-life events in the child's life.

- **Calculators to check word problems.** Ask the student to use a calculator to check computations made in answering assigned word problems.

Use of Special Materials in Math

Some children with ADHD benefit from using special materials to help them complete their math assignments, including the following:

- **Number lines.** Provide number lines for the child to use when computing whole numbers.
- **Manipulatives.** Use manipulatives to help students gain basic computation skills such as counting poker chips when adding single-digit numbers.
- **Graph paper.** Ask the child to use graph paper to help organize columns when adding, subtracting, multiplying, or dividing whole numbers.

Organizational and Study Skills Useful for Academic Instruction of Children With ADHD

Many students with ADHD are easily distracted and have difficulty focusing their attention on assigned tasks. However, the following practices can help children with ADHD improve their organization of homework and other daily assignments:

- **Designate one teacher as the student's advisor or coordinator.** This teacher will regularly review the student's progress through progress reports submitted by other teachers and will act as the liaison between home and school. Permit the student to meet with this advisor on a regular basis (e.g., Monday morning) to plan and organize for the week and to review progress and problems from the past week.
- **Assignment notebooks.** Provide the child with an assignment notebook to help organize homework and other seatwork.
- **Color-coded folders.** Provide the child with color-coded folders to help organize assignments for different academic subjects (e.g., reading, mathematics, social science, and science).
- **Work with a homework partner.** Assign the child a partner to help record homework and other seatwork in the assignment notebook and file worksheets and other papers in the proper folders.

- **Clean out desks and bookbags.** Ask the child to periodically sort through and clean out his or her desk, bookbag, and other special places where written assignments are stored.
- **Visual aids as reminders of subject material.** Use posters in the classroom, banners, charts, lists, pie graphs, and diagrams situated throughout the classroom to remind students of the subject material being learned.

Assisting Students With ADHD With Time Management

Children with ADHD often have difficulty finishing their assignments on time and can thus benefit from special materials and practices that help them to improve their time-management skills, including the following:

- **Use a clock or wristwatch.** Teach the child how to read and use a clock or wristwatch to manage time when completing assigned work.
- **Use a calendar.** Teach the child how to read and use a calendar to schedule assignments.
- **Practice sequencing activities.** Provide the child with supervised opportunities to break down a long assignment into a sequence of short, interrelated activities.
- **Create a daily activity schedule.** Tape a schedule of planned daily activities to the child's desk.

Helpful Study Skills for Students With ADHD

Children with ADHD often have difficulty in learning how to study effectively on their own. The following strategies may assist ADHD students in developing the study skills necessary for academic success:

- **Adapt worksheets.** Teach a child how to adapt instructional worksheets. For example, help a child fold his or her reading worksheet to reveal only one question at a time. The child can also use a blank piece of paper to cover the other questions on the page.
- **Venn diagrams.** Teach a child how to use Venn diagrams to help illustrate and organize key concepts in reading, mathematics, or other academic subjects.

- **Note-taking skills.** Teach a child with ADHD how to take notes when organizing key academic concepts that he or she has learned, perhaps with the use of a program such as *Skills for School Success* (Archer & Gleason, 2002).
- **Checklist of frequent mistakes.** Provide the child with a checklist of mistakes that he or she frequently makes in written assignments (e.g., punctuation or capitalization errors), mathematics (e.g., addition or subtraction errors), or other academic subjects. Teach the child how to use this list when proofreading his or her work at home and school.
- **Checklist of homework supplies.** Provide the child with a checklist that identifies categories of items needed for homework assignments (e.g., books, pencils, and homework assignment sheets).
- **Uncluttered workspace.** Teach a child with ADHD how to prepare an uncluttered workspace to complete assignments. For example, instruct the child to clear away unnecessary books or other materials *before* beginning his or her seatwork.
- **Monitor homework assignments.** Keep track of how well your students with ADHD complete their assigned homework. Discuss and resolve with them and their parents any problems in completing these assignments. For example, evaluate the difficulty of the assignments and how long the children spend on their homework each night. Keep in mind that the *quality*, rather than the *quantity*, of homework assigned is the most important issue. While doing homework is an important part of developing study skills, it should be used to reinforce skills and to review material learned in class, rather than to present, in advance, large amounts of material that is new to the student.

Conclusion

For individuals with ADHD, one of the most critical areas in which to offer support is in the school arena. This is where most children with ADHD experience the greatest difficulty. That is because schools require great skill in the areas where students with ADHD are the weakest: attention, executive function, and memory. Although ADHD does not interfere with the ability to learn, it does wreak havoc on performance. Behavior problems, which usually get the most attention, may actually be by-products of the school environment and ADHD. These usually occur when tasks are too long, too hard, or lack interest. Many behavior problems can be avoided or lessened by adapting the school setting to fit the needs of the student.

In the school arena, ADHD is an educational performance problem. When little or nothing is done to help children with ADHD improve their performance, over time they will show academic achievement problems. This underachievement is not the result of an inability to learn. It is caused by the cumulative effects of missing important blocks of information and skill development that build from lesson to lesson and from one school year to the next.

A student with ADHD can have difficulty in any number of academic areas and with critical academic skills. Thus it is extremely important that the school and parents work together to design an appropriate educational program for the student. This program needs to include the accommodations, modifications, and other services necessary to support the student academically and promote successful learning and appropriate behavior.

Step IX

Implementing Behavioral Intervention Techniques

The second major component of effective instruction for children with ADHD involves the use of *behavioral interventions*. Exhibiting behavior that resembles that of younger children, children with ADHD often do not act age appropriate and have difficulty learning how to control their impulsiveness and hyperactivity. They may have problems forming friendships with other children in the class and may have difficulty thinking through the social consequences of their actions.

The purpose of behavioral interventions is to assist students in displaying the behaviors that are most conducive to their own learning as well as that of classmates. Well-managed classrooms prevent many disciplinary problems and provide an environment that is most favorable for learning. When a teacher's time must be spent interacting with students whose behaviors are not focused on the lesson being presented, less time is available for assisting other students. Behavioral interventions should be viewed as an opportunity for teaching in the most effective and efficient manner, rather than as an opportunity for punishment.

Effective Behavioral Intervention Techniques

Effective teachers use a number of behavioral intervention techniques to help students learn how to control their behavior. Perhaps the most important and effective of these is *verbal reinforcement* of appropriate behavior. The most common form of verbal reinforcement is *praise* given to a student when he or she begins and completes an activity or exhibits a particular desired behavior. Simple phrases such as "good job" encourage a child to act appropriately. Effective teachers praise not just children with ADHD frequently, but *all* children frequently, and look for a behavior to praise before, and not after, a child gets off task. The following strategies provide some guidance regarding the use of praise:

- **Define the appropriate behavior while giving praise.** Praise should be specific for the positive behavior displayed by the student: The comments should focus on what the student did right and should include exactly what part(s) of the student's behavior was desirable. Rather than praising a student for not disturbing the class, for example, a teacher should praise him or her for quietly completing a math lesson on time.
- **Give praise immediately.** The sooner that approval is given regarding appropriate behavior, the more likely the student will repeat it.
- **Vary the statements given as praise.** The comments used by teachers to praise appropriate behavior should vary; when students hear the same praise statement repeated over and over, it may lose its value.
- **Be consistent and sincere with praise.** Appropriate behavior should receive consistent praise. Consistency among teachers with respect to desired behavior is important in order to avoid confusion on the part of students with ADHD. Similarly, students will notice when teachers give insincere praise, and this insincerity will make praise less effective.

It is important to keep in mind that the most effective teachers focus their behavioral intervention strategies on *praise* rather than on *punishment*. Negative consequences may temporarily change behavior, but they rarely change attitudes and may actually increase the frequency and intensity of inappropriate behavior by rewarding misbehaving students with attention. Moreover, punishment may only teach children what not to do; it does not provide children with the skills that they need to do what is expected. Positive reinforcement produces the changes in attitudes that will shape a student's behavior over the long term.

In addition to verbal reinforcement, the following set of generalized behavioral intervention techniques has proven helpful with students with ADHD as well:

- **Selectively ignore inappropriate behavior.** It is sometimes helpful for teachers to selectively ignore inappropriate behavior. This technique is particularly useful when the behavior is unintentional or unlikely to recur or is intended solely to gain the attention of teachers or classmates without disrupting the classroom or interfering with the learning of others.
- **Remove nuisance items.** Teachers often find that certain objects (e.g., rubber bands and toys) distract the attention of students with ADHD in the classroom. The removal of nuisance items is generally most effective after the student has been given the choice of putting it away immediately and then fails to do so.
- **Provide calming manipulatives.** While some toys and other objects can be distracting for both the students with ADHD and peers in the classroom, some children with ADHD can benefit from having access to objects that can be manipulated quietly. Manipulatives may help children gain some needed sensory input while still attending to the lesson.
- **Allow for "escape valve" outlets.** Permitting students with ADHD to leave class for a moment, perhaps on an errand (e.g., returning a book to the library), can be an effective means of settling them down and allowing them to return to the room ready to concentrate.
- **Activity reinforcement.** Students receive activity reinforcement when they are encouraged to perform a less desirable behavior before a preferred one.
- **Hurdle helping.** Teachers can offer encouragement, support, and assistance to prevent students from becoming frustrated with an assignment. This help can take many forms, from enlisting a peer for support to supplying additional materials or information.
- **Parent conferences.** Parents/guardians have a critical role in the education of students, and this axiom may be particularly true for those with ADHD. As such, parents must be included as partners in planning for the student's success. Partnering with parents entails including parental input in behavioral intervention strategies, maintaining frequent communication

between parents and teachers, and collaborating in monitoring the student's progress.

- **Peer mediation.** Members of a student's peer group can positively impact the behavior of students with ADHD. Many schools now have formalized peer mediation programs, in which students receive training in order to manage disputes involving their classmates.

Effective teachers also use *behavioral prompts* with their students. These prompts help remind students about expectations for their learning and behavior in the classroom. Three that may be particularly helpful are the following:

1. **Visual cues.** Establish simple, nonintrusive visual cues to remind the child to remain on task. For example, you can smile at the child while looking him or her in the eye, or you can hold out your hand, palm down, near the child.
2. **Proximity control.** When talking to a child, move to where the child is standing or sitting. Your physical proximity to the child will help the child to focus and pay attention to what you are saying.
3. **Hand gestures.** Use hand signals to communicate privately with a child with ADHD. For example, ask the child to raise his or her hand every time you ask a question. A closed fist can signal that the child knows the answer; an open palm can signal that he or she does not know the answer. You would call on the child to answer only when he or she makes a fist.

In some instances, children with ADHD benefit from instruction designed to help students learn how to manage their own behavior:

- **Social skills classes.** Teach children with ADHD appropriate social skills using a structured class. For example, you can ask the children to role-play and model different solutions to common social problems. It is critical to provide for the generalization of these skills including structured opportunities for the children to use the social skills that they learn. Offering such classes, or experiences, to the general school population can positively affect the school climate.
- **Problem-solving sessions.** Discuss how to resolve social conflicts. Conduct impromptu discussions with one student or with a small group of students where the conflict arises. In this setting, ask two children who are arguing about a game to discuss how to settle their differences. Encourage the chil-

dren to resolve their problem by talking to each other in a supervised setting.

For many children with ADHD, *functional behavioral assessments* and *positive behavioral interventions* and supports including behavioral contracts and management plans, tangible rewards, or token economy systems are helpful in teaching them how to manage their own behavior. Because students' individual needs are different, it is important for teachers, along with the family and other involved professionals, to evaluate whether these practices are appropriate for their classrooms. Examples of these techniques, along with steps to follow when using them, include the following:

- **Functional Behavioral Assessment (FBA).** FBA is a systematic process for describing problem behavior and identifying the environmental factors and surrounding events associated with problem behavior. The team that works closely with the child exhibiting problem behavior (a) observes the behavior and identifies and defines its problematic characteristics, (b) identifies which actions or events precede and follow the behavior, and (c) determines how often the behavior occurs. The results of the FBA should be used to develop an effective and efficient intervention and support plan (Gable et al., 1997).
- **Positive Behavioral Interventions and Supports (PBIS).** This method is an application of a behaviorally based systems approach that is grounded in research regarding behavior in the context of the settings in which it occurs. Using this method, schools, families, and communities work to design effective environments to improve behavior. The goal of PBIS is to eliminate problem behavior, to replace it with more appropriate behavior, and to increase a person's skills and opportunities for an enhanced quality of life (Todd, Horner, Sugai, & Sprague, 1999).
- **Behavioral contracts and management plans.** Identify specific academic or behavioral goals for the child with ADHD, along with behavior that needs to change and strategies for responding to inappropriate behavior. Work with the child to cooperatively identify appropriate goals such as completing homework assignments on time and obeying safety rules on the school playground. Take the time to ensure that the child agrees that his or her goals are important to master. Behavioral contracts and management plans are typically

used with individual children, as opposed to entire classes, and should be prepared with input from parents.

- **Tangible rewards.** Use tangible rewards to reinforce appropriate behavior. These rewards can include stickers such as "happy faces" or sports team emblems or privileges such as extra time on the computer or lunch with the teacher. Children should be involved in the selection of the reward. If children are invested in the reward, they are more likely to work for it.

- **Token economy systems.** Use token economy systems to motivate a child to achieve a goal identified in a behavioral contract (Barkley, 1990a, 1990b). For example, a child can earn points for each homework assignment completed on time. In some cases, students also lose points for each homework assignment not completed on time. After earning a specified number of points, the student receives a tangible reward such as extra time on a computer or a "free" period on Friday afternoon. Token economy systems are often used for entire classrooms, as opposed to solely for individual students.

- **Self-management systems.** Train students to monitor and evaluate their own behavior without constant feedback from the teacher. In a typical self-management system, the teacher identifies behaviors that will be managed by a student and provides a written rating scale that includes the performance criteria for each rating. The teacher and student separately rate student behavior during an activity and compare ratings. The student earns points if the ratings match or are within one point and receives no points if ratings are more than one point apart; points are exchanged for privileges. With time, the teacher involvement is removed, and the student becomes responsible for self-monitoring (DuPaul & Stoner, 2002).

Behavior Interventions—Examples to Share With Parents/Guardians

Behavior Intervention for Parents to Use #1—Be an Executive

Provide structure, routines, assistive devices, external supports, and guides.

Think of the executive as the boss who creates a work environment in which all the workers know what they have to do to do their jobs appropriately. The boss also provides the necessary structure for them to do so. Performance expectations and company rules are clear. The executive supervises and directs but does not overmanage or micromanage. Children who have difficulty with planning, thinking, organizing, concentrating, and self-monitoring need to have systems in place to guide and direct them. Parents and teachers need to be the executives in the child's life.

Examples include the following:

- Make your expectations clear. Say, "I expect you to. . ."
- Try to do things at the same time every day—homework, playtime, recreation, bedtime. Post the schedule on the fridge. When making schedule changes, give advance warning as much as possible.
- Have simple systems for organization—where to keep possessions and needed items such as backpacks, gym clothes, pens, and so on.
- Use homework organizers, notebook organizers, day planners, weekly planners, computers, or even laptops—when called for.
- Do backpack cleaning and notebook organization once a week.

Understand that you and your child's teachers will need to provide much more direct supervision than seems necessary for the chronological age. Remember, ADHD is a developmental disability, so these youth usually fall short of age expectations.

Behavior Intervention for Parents to Use #2— Develop Behavior Management Strategies

Use positive attention, rules and consequences, and formal systems such as contracts and charts.

The main goal of all behavior management strategies is to increase the child's appropriate behavior and decrease inappropriate behavior. The best way to influence any behavior is to pay attention to it. Thus the best way to increase a desirable behavior is to *catch the child being good.*

How do you make the bulk of your interactions positive and yet still provide discipline? The answer is with thought and planning. Effective parents (and teachers) know ahead of time what behaviors are acceptable and not acceptable. They know what issues they are willing to negotiate and what issues, like safety, are nonnegotiable. In a nutshell, do not sweat the small stuff, and do not ignore the good stuff no matter how small.

Much of behavior management is about changing what you do. House rules set by the parents (or the classroom rules) need to be carefully designed. First, you want to structure them so that the child will be able to meet the expectations. In other words, you do not wait for a behavior to happen or not happen. You change what happens *before* the behavior—head it off at the pass, so to speak. For instance, if the child constantly forgets things for school, design a system for where to put things so they get picked up on the way out the door.

Your son or daughter needs to know ahead of time what behavior is expected. He or she also needs to know what the consequences will be for behaving (following the rules) or for misbehaving (breaking the rules). Consequences are given as soon as possible. Give far more positive consequences and rewards than punishment. Children who hear too much negative feedback often become oppositional or depressed. Managing behavior thoughtfully, without a lot of reaction, especially undue punishment or criticism, helps to prevent unwanted side effects of poorly managed AD/HD.

Some families need to use formal behavior management systems. These include charts or contracts. The difference between the two is simple.

Generally, *contracts* are used during early to midadolescence. In a contract, the involved parties (usually the parents and child, or teacher and student) talk about certain chores or obligations that the youth will fulfill. They draw up an agreement. The youth receives certain agreed-upon privileges or rewards for meeting the terms of the contract.

Charts are usually used for children ages eleven or younger. A chart lists behaviors that the child must display. Points are given or taken away depending on the child's behavior. Accumulated points may be traded for rewards.

If you decide to make a behavior modification chart, you may wish to follow these three simple steps:

- Make a list of problematic behaviors or ones that need improving.
- Select three to five behaviors from the list. Review the list and, with input from your child, select the behaviors to work on. Pick behaviors that occur on a daily or frequent basis, such as doing homework, going to bed on time, being respectful to all family members, or doing chores.
- Create a reward system. Assign a point value to each listed behavior. Throughout the day, give points for appropriate behavior. At the end of the day or week, your child can "cash

in" points for rewards or privileges that have been agreed upon in advance.

In order for rewards to work, they must have value to the child. Since children with ADHD tend to become disinterested in the same thing over time, the rewards usually need to be changed frequently to have value.

Punishment

Children and teens with ADHD respond best to motivation and positive reinforcement. It is best to avoid punishment. When punishment is necessary, use it sparingly and with sensitivity. It is important that you and your child's teachers respond to the inappropriate behavior without anger and in a matter-of-fact way. Your child needs to be taught to replace inappropriate with appropriate behavior.

Time-Out

When your child is misbehaving or out of control, time-out can be an effective way to manage the problem. Time-out means that your child is sent for a short period to a previously agreed-upon place— usually out of the main hub, like a special chair or area of a room. In general, he or she stays in time-out and must be quiet for three to five minutes. The time-out place should not be a traumatic place such as a closet or dark basement. The purpose of time-out is to provide a cooling off place where your child can regain control.

Time-out works best with preadolescent kids. You can also use time-out with teens. Usually that means asking your teen to go to another room alone until he or she calms down.

Behavior Intervention for Parents to Use #3— Use Problem Solving

Develop skills in the art of negotiation, give and take, and conflict resolution through peaceful means.

Problem solving helps take the reaction out of parenting. It is results oriented. If your child is mature enough, involve him or her in this process. Good problem solving has three parts:

1. accurately defining the problem,
2. coming up with workable solutions, and
3. evaluating results and trying something else, if necessary.

Very often, people spend a lot of time solving the wrong problem. It is important to analyze problem areas. Pay attention to the facts and not the emotions of the situation. Brainstorm to find possible solutions. Put down all ideas that come to mind. Evaluate them. Pick the one that seems most likely to work. Go back to the drawing board if it does not. This approach helps to stop conflict from escalating.

For example, suppose your child argues when you ask him or her to do a chore. While it appears as if arguing is the problem, actually, that behavior might be the result of some problem with the request to do chores. Instead of focusing on the arguing, direct your attention to the chore and to what that problem is. For instance, do you have a regular chore schedule? Are expectations clear? Does the child understand all the task expectations? Is there a definite time line? To some children, picking up the room means moving a couple of things out of the way.

Once you clearly define the problem, then you can brainstorm for a workable solution. Let us say your child understands all aspects of the chore, but it still does not get done without your nagging or threatening. Come up with a plan where the child knows exactly what to do by when. Decide if reminders will be given. Give a reward for on-time chore completion. Give a bonus if the chore is done ahead of time. Penalize the child if the chore is not done on time, but do not nag. Take action. Do not react. Make not doing the chore the child's problem and not yours.

Behavior Intervention for Parents to Use # 4— Use Good Communication Skills

Say what you mean in a firm, loving way. Practice listening without judgment and discussion without attack. *Recognize that your child with ADHD has trouble listening. Be brief and to the point.*

Screaming, yelling, speaking through clenched teeth, stamping feet, throwing things, finger pointing, and making threats are violent forms of communication. These escalate problems, as do put-downs, sarcasm, lecturing, preaching, and name-calling. When we are using good communication skills, we

- let the speaker finish,
- concentrate on what is being said,
- show interest,
- avoid judgment,
- eliminate putdowns,
- express our agreement, and

- use praise.

Problem solving and good communication help to eliminate some of the oppositional and hostile encounters that often accompany the disorder of ADHD.

Conclusion

As parents and teachers know, ADHD can cause significant inappropriate behavior. Frequent complaints include failure to follow rules, listen to commands, complete tasks, delay gratification, or control impulse. In addition, some youth may be aggressive or anxious. These symptoms lead to their own set of problems such as fighting or avoiding tasks. It is very easy for everyone involved—the child, the parents, and the teacher(s)—to be worn down into a pattern of negative, and sometimes hostile, interactions. This cycle, however, can be broken, and different, more positive interactions and behavior patterns can be developed. Knowing more about behavior and about how to support behavior that is positive and appropriate is extremely useful information for any parent or teacher of a child with ADHD.

Step X

Implementing Classroom Accommodation and Modification Techniques

The third component of a strategy for effectively educating children with ADHD involves physical *classroom accommodations and modifications*. Children with ADHD often have difficulty adjusting to the structured environment of a classroom, determining what is important, and focusing on their assigned work. They are easily distracted by other children or by nearby activities in the classroom. As a result, many children with ADHD benefit from accommodations or modifications that reduce distractions in the classroom environment and help them to stay on task and learn. Certain accommodations within the physical and learning environments of the classroom can benefit children with ADHD.

Special Classroom Seating Arrangements for ADHD Students

One of the most common accommodations that can be made to the physical environment of the classroom involves determining where a child with ADHD will sit. Three special seating assignments may be especially useful:

- **Seat the child near the teacher.** Assign the child a seat near your desk or the front of the room. This seating assignment provides opportunities for you to monitor and reinforce the child's on-task behavior. Be careful that the seating does not prevent the child from viewing the other students in the room.

- **Seat the child near a student role model.** Assign the child a seat near a student role model. This seat arrangement provides opportunity for children to work cooperatively and to learn from their peers in the class.
- **Provide low-distraction work areas.** As space permits, teachers should make available a quiet, distraction-free room or area for quiet study time and test taking. Students should be directed to this room or area privately and discreetly in order to avoid the appearance of punishment.

Instructional Tools and the Physical Learning Environment

Skilled teachers use special instructional tools to modify the classroom learning environment and accommodate the special needs of their students with ADHD. They also monitor the physical environment, keeping in mind the needs of these children. The following tools and techniques may be helpful:

- **Pointers.** Teach the child to use a pointer to help visually track written words on a page. For example, provide the child with a bookmark to help him or her follow along when students are taking turns reading aloud.
- **Egg timers.** Note for the children the time at which the lesson is starting and the time at which it will conclude. Set a timer to indicate to children how much time remains in the lesson and place the timer at the front of the classroom; the children can check the timer to see how much time remains. Interim prompts can be used as well. For instance, children can monitor their own progress during a thirty-minute lesson if the timer is set for ten minutes three times.
- **Classroom lights.** Turning the classroom lights on and off prompts children that the noise level in the room is too high and they should be quiet. This practice can also be used to signal that it is time to begin preparing for the next lesson.
- **Music.** Play music on a tape recorder or chords on a piano to prompt children that they are too noisy. In addition, playing

different types of music on a tape recorder communicates to children what level of activity is appropriate for a particular lesson. For example, play quiet classical music for quiet activities done independently and jazz for active group activities. However, be aware that for some children with ADHD, music can be distracting. Therefore, use your best professional judgment when determining whether to using music as a strategy.

- **Proper use of furniture.** The desk and chair used by children with ADHD need to be the right size; if they are not, the child will be more inclined to squirm and fidget. A general rule of thumb is that a child should be able to put his or her elbows on the surface of the desk and have his or her chin fit comfortably in the palm of the hand.

Conclusion

Classroom Management Techniques for Students With ADHD: A Step-by-Step Guide for Educators has outlined a series of instructional strategies that have proven to be successful in educating children with ADHD. However, it should be emphasized that these techniques are also highly useful for *all* children. The three main components of a successful strategy for educating children with ADHD are *academic instruction, behavioral interventions,* and *classroom accommodations and modifications.* By incorporating techniques from these three areas into their everyday instructional and classroom management practices, teachers will be empowered to improve both the academic performance and the behavior of their students with ADHD. In doing so, teachers will create an enhanced learning environment for all students.

Glossary

Accommodation—The use of materials and techniques that allow individuals to finish school or work tasks with greater ease and effectiveness

Adderall—One of the central nervous system (CNS) stimulants; it is a stimulant drug used to improve attention span and decrease impulsivity

Adult ADHD—The continuation of ADHD symptoms into adulthood

Alternative Education Placement (AEP)—An alternative classroom setting used to improve classroom behavior and to address needs that cannot be met in a regular classroom setting

Americans with Disabilities Act (ADA)—A federal law that gives civil rights protections to individuals with disabilities similar to those provided to individuals on the basis of race, color, sex, national origin, age, and religion; it guarantees equal opportunity for individuals with disabilities in public accommodations, employment, transportation, state and local government services, and telecommunications

Amphetamines—Drugs used to stimulate the brain; in children, can be used to treat hyperactivity

Antidepressants—Normally, the second-line treatment for ADHD, it is medication used to improve mood for individuals with depression but can be used to treat hyperactivity

Anxiety—A feeling of apprehension and fear characterized by physical symptoms such as palpitations, sweating, and feelings of stress

Assistive Technology—Equipment that enhances the ability of students and employees to be more efficient and successful

Attention—The ability to focus selectively on a selected stimulus, sustaining that focus and shifting it at will; it is the ability to concentrate

Attentional—Relating to attention

Attention Deficit Hyperactivity Disorder (ADHD)—A developmental and behavioral disorder marked by inattention, hyperactivity and impulsivity that is inappropriate for the child's age level; a person can be predominantly inattentive (often referred to as ADD), predominantly hyperactive-impulsive, or a combination of these two

Attention Deficit Disorder (ADD)—Another term for the predominantly inattentive type of ADHD, which is marked by inattention, but does not include hyperactivity or impulsivity

Behavior Intervention Plan (BIP)—A plan that includes positive strategies, program modifications, and supplementary aids and supports that address a student's disruptive behaviors and allows the child to be educated in the least restrictive environment (LRE)

Behavior Modification—The use of basic learning techniques such as conditioning, biofeedback, reinforcement, or aversion therapy to alter human behavior

Behavior Therapy—A treatment program that involves substituting desirable behavior responses for undesirable ones

Brain—That part of the central nervous system that is located within the cranium (skull); the brain functions as the primary receiver, organizer, and distributor of information for the body

Chronic—This important term in medicine comes from the Greek *chronos*, time, and means lasting a long time

Cognitive—Pertaining to cognition, the process of knowing and, more precisely, the process of being aware, knowing, thinking, learning, and judging

Comorbidity—The coexistence of two or more disorders

Combined Type ADHD—Most common type of ADHD, which is marked by symptoms of inattention, hyperactivity, and impulsiveness

Concerta—One of the central nervous system (CNS) stimulants; it goes by the generic name methylphenidate

Cylert—A central nervous system stimulant indicated for the treatment of ADHD

Dexedrine—One of the central nervous system (CNS) stimulants; it goes by the generic name dextroamphetamine

Dexmethylphenidate—One of the central nervous system (CNS) stimulants; it goes by the brand name Focalin

DextroStat—One of the central nervous system (CNS) stimulants; it goes by the generic name dextroamphetamine

Diagnosis—The identification of a disorder

Differential diagnosis—The process of determining the probability of one disorder versus another

DSM-IV—The fourth edition of *Diagnostic and Statistical Manual of Mental Disorders*

DSM-IV-TR—*Diagnostic and Statistical Manual of Mental Disorders, Fourth Edition, Text Revision*; manual published by the American Psychiatric Association that sets criteria for the diagnosis of neurobiologic and other psychiatric disorders such as ADHD

Family—A group of individuals related by blood or marriage or by a feeling of closeness

Free Appropriate Public Education (FAPE)—A requirement of IDEA; all children with disabilities must receive special education services and related services at no cost

Focalin—One of the central nervous system (CNS) stimulants; it goes by the generic name dexmethylphenidate

Functional Behavioral Assessment (FBA)—A problem-solving process for addressing student problem behavior that uses techniques to identify what triggers a given behavior(s) and to select interventions that directly address them

Genetic—Pertaining to genes and genetic information

Hyperactivity—Highly or excessively active behavior that characterizes a child with ADHD

Impairment—To cause to diminish, as in strength, value, or quality

Impulsiveness—The inclination to act inappropriately based on an impulse rather than on a considered decision

Inattention—The inability to focus the attention and keep it focused on a task or topic that characterizes a child with ADD or combined type ADHD

Individuals with Disabilities Education Act of 2004 (IDEA 2004)— The law that guarantees all children with disabilities access to a free and appropriate public education

Insomnia—The inability to fall sleep, which is an occasional side effect of stimulant treatment of ADHD

Intervention—The act of intervening, interfering or interceding with the intent of modifying the outcome

Learning Disability (LD)—A disorder that affects a person's ability to either interpret what they see and hear or to link information from different parts of the brain; it may also be referred to as a learning disorder or a learning difference

Least Restrictive Environment (LRE)—A learning plan that provides the most possible time in the regular classroom setting

Local Education Agency (LEA)—A public board of education or other public authority within a state that maintains administrative control of public elementary or secondary schools in a city, county, township, school district or other political subdivision of a state

Medication—A drug or medicine

Methylphenidate—A class of medications called central nervous system (CNS) stimulants that work by changing the amounts of certain natural substances in the brain

Multimodal Treatment Study of ADHD—Study conducted by the National Institute of Mental Health (NIMH) and cosponsored by the U.S. Department of Education to identify and compare benefits of different treatment modalities for ADHD; one of the largest and longest running clinical ADHD trials to date; first results were released in late 1999; periodic updates are ongoing

Neurological—Having to do with the function of the brain

Neurotransmitter—A chemical in the brain that facilitates the transmission of nerve impulses, which are thought to play a role in controlling behavior

NIMH—Stands for the National Institute of Mental Health, one of the National Institutes of Health in the United States whose mission is to "provide national leadership dedicated to understanding, treating, and preventing mental illnesses through basic research on the brain and behavior, and through clinical, epidemiological, and services research"

No Child Left Behind (NCLB)—The No Child Left Behind Act of 2001 is the most recent reauthorization of the Elementary and Secondary Education act of 1965

Office of Special Education Programs (OSEP)—An office of the U.S. Department of Education whose goal is to improve results for children with disabilities (ages birth through twenty-one by providing leadership and financial support to assist states and local districts

Other Health Impairments (OHI)—A disability category under IDEA 2004, it pertains to students with limited strength, vitality or alertness, due to chronic or acute health problems (e.g., asthma, ADHD, diabetes, or a heart condition)

Pediatric—Pertaining to children

Pharmacological—Pertaining to the science of drugs, including their composition, uses, and effects

Predominantly Hyperactive-Impulsive Type ADHD—A form of ADHD in which the child exhibits both hyperactive and impulsive behavior, but does not have difficulty paying attention

Response to Intervention (RTI)—Under IDEA 2004, school districts can use this model (also called the Three-Tiered Model) as an alternative to the discrepancy model to determine whether a student has a learning disability

Ritalin—One of the central nervous system (CNS) stimulants; it goes by the generic name methylphenidate

Section 504—The law that prohibits discrimination against individuals with disabilities

Self-Advocacy—The development of specific skills and understandings that enable children and adults to explain their specific learning disabilities to others and cope positively with the attitudes of peers, parents, teachers, and employers

Side Effects—Problems that occur when treatment goes beyond the desired effect or problems that occur in addition to the desired therapeutic effect

Special Education (SPED)—Services offered to children who possess one or more of the following disabilities: specific learning disabilities, speech or language impairments, mental retardation, emotional disturbance, multiple disabilities, hearing impairments, orthopedic impairments, visual impairments, autism, combined deafness and blindness, traumatic brain injury, and other health impairments

Specific Learning Disability (SLD)—The official term used in federal legislation to refer to difficulty in certain areas of learning, rather than in all areas of learning

Stimulant—A class of medications that stimulate the production of the neurotransmitter dopamine to help people with ADHD to focus their minds; these are the most common treatment for ADHD

Strattera—The first medication approved for the treatment of ADHD that is a nonstimulant

Tics—A habitual spasmodic muscular movement or contraction, usually of the face or extremities

References

Abramowitz, A. J., Eckstrand, D., O'Leary, S. G., & Dulcan, M. K. (1992). ADHD children's responses to stimulant medication and two intensities of a behavioral intervention. *Behavior Modification, 16,* 193–203.

American Academy of Pediatrics. (2000). Clinical practice guideline: Diagnosis and evaluation of the child with attention-deficit/hyperactivity disorder. *Pediatrics, 105*(5), 1158–1170.

American Psychiatric Association [APA] (2000). *Publication Manual of the American Psychological Association,* 5th ed. Washington, DC: Author

American Psychological Association (2001). Clinical practice guideline: Treatment of the school-aged child with attention deficit/hyperactivity disorder [Electronic version]. *Pediatrics, 108,* 1033–1044.

American Psychiatric Association (APA). (2000). *Diagnostic and statistical manual of mental disorders* (4th ed.). Washington, DC: Author.

American Psychiatric Association [APA] (2000). *Publication Manual of the American Psychological Association,* 5th ed. Washington, DC: American Psychological Association.

Anderson, J. C., Williams, S. C., McGee, R., & Silva, P. A. (1987). *DSM-III* disorders in preadolescent children: Prevalence in a large sample from the general population. *Archives of General Psychiatry, 44,* 69–76.

Archer, A., & Gleason, M. (2002). *Skills for school success: Book 5.* North Billerica, MA: Curriculum Associates, Inc.

Barkley, R. A. (1990a). *Attention deficit hyperactivity disorder: A handbook for diagnosis and treatment.* New York: Guilford Press.

Barkley, R. A. (1990b). Comprehensive evaluation of attention deficit disorder with and without hyperactivity as defined by research criteria. *Journal of Consulting and Clinical Psychology, 58,* 775–789.

Barkley, R. A. (1997). Behavioral inhibition, sustained attention, and executive functions: Constructing a unifying theory of ADHD. *Psychological Bulletin, 121*(1), 65–94.

Barkley, R. A. (September, 1998a). Attention-deficit hyperactivity disorder. *Scientific American, 279,* 3.

Barkley, R. A. (1998b). *Handbook of attention deficit hyperactivity disorder* (2nd ed.). New York: Guilford Press.

Barkley, R. A. (2000). *Taking charge of ADHD: The complete, authoritative guide for parents* (Rev. ed.). New York: Guilford.

Barkley, R. A., DuPaul, G., & O'Connor, D. (1999). Stimulants. In J. S. Werry & M. G. Aman (Eds.), *Practitioner's guide to psychoactive drugs for children and adolescents* (2nd ed.). New York: Plenum.

Bird, H. R., Canino, G., Rubio-Stipec, M., Gould, M. S., Ribera, J., & Sesman, M. (1988). Estimates of the prevalence of childhood maladjustment in a community survey in Puerto Rico: The use of combined measures. *Archives of General Psychiatry, 45,* 1120–1126.

Burt, S. A., Krueger, R. F., McGue, M., & Iacono, W. G. (2001). Sources of covariation among attention-deficit/hyperactivity disorder, oppositional defiant disorder, and conduct disorder: The importance of shared environment. *Journal of Abnormal Psychology, 110,* 516–525.

Cantwell, D. P., & Baker, L. (1991). Association between attention deficit-hyperactivity disorder and learning disorders. *Journal of Learning Disabilities, 24,* 88–95.

Carlson, C. L., Pelham, W. E., Jr., Milich, R., & Dixon, J. (1992). Single and combined effects of methylphenidate and behavior therapy on the classroom performance of children with attention-deficit hyperactivity disorder. *Journal of Abnormal Child Psychology, 20,* 213–232.

Castellanos, F.X., & Swanson, I.M. (2002). Biological underpinnings of ADHD. In S. Sandberg (Ed.), *Hyperactivity and attention disorders of childhood* (2nd ed.). Cambridge, England: Cambridge University Press.

DuPaul, G. J., & Stoner, G. (1994). *ADHD in the schools: Assessment and intervention strategies.* New York: Guilford Press.

DuPaul, G. J., & Stoner, G. (2002). Interventions for attention problems. In M. R. Shinn, H. M. Walker, & G. Stoner (Eds.), *Interventions for academic and behavior problems II: Preventive and remedial approaches* (pp. 913–938). Bethesda, MD: National Association of School Psychologists.

Dykman, R. A., Akerman, P. T., & Raney, T. J. (1994). *Assessment and Characteristics of Children with Attention Deficit Disorder.* Prepared for the Office of Special Education Programs, Office of Special Education and Rehabilitative Services, U.S. Department of Education.

Edwards, J. H. (2002). Evidenced-based treatment for child ADHD: "Real world" practice implications. *Journal of Mental Health Counseling, 24*(2), 126–139.

Esser, G., Schmidt, M. H., & Woemer, W. (1990). Epidemiology and course of psychiatric disorders in school-age children: Results of a longitudinal study. *Journal of Child Psychology and Psychiatry, 31,* 243–263. Castellanos, F.X., & Swanson, I.M. (2002). Biological underpinnings of ADHD. In S. Sandberg (Ed.), *Hyperactivity and attention disorders of childhood* (2nd ed.). Cambridge, England: Cambridge University Press.

Friend, M. (2005). *Special education: Contemporary perspectives for school professionals.* Boston, MA: Allyn and Bacon.

Forness, S. R., & Kavale, K. A. (2001). ADHD and a return to the medical model of special education. *Education and Treatment of Children, 24*(3), 224–247.

Forness, S. R., Kavale, K. A., & San Miguel, S. (1998). The psychiatric comorbidity hypothesis revisited. *Learning Disability Quarterly, 21,* 203–207.

Gable, R. A., Sugai, G. M., Lewis, T. J., Nelson, J. R., Cheney, D., Safran, S. P., et al. (1997). *Individual and systemic approaches to collaboration and consultation.* Reston, VA: Council for Children with Behavioral Disorders.

Gargiulo, R. M. (2004). *Special education in contemporary society: An introduction to exceptionality.* Belmont, CA: Thomson-Wadsworth.

Goldman, L. S., Genel, M., Bezman, R., & Slanetz, P. J. (1998). Diagnosis and treatment of attention-deficit/hyperactivity disorder in children and adolescents. *Journal of the American Medical Association, 279*(14), 1100–1107.

Heward, W. L. (2006). *Exceptional children: An introduction to special education* (8th ed.). Upper Saddle River, NJ: Pearson Education.

Hinshaw, S. P., Owens, E. B., Wells, K. C., Kraemer, H. C., Abikoff, H. B., Arnold, L. E., et al. (2000). Family processes and treatment outcome in the MTA: Negative/ineffective parenting practices in relation to multimodal treatment. *Journal of Abnormal Child Psychology, 28*(6), 555–568.

Holt, S. B., & O'Tuel, F. S. (1989). The effect of sustained silent reading and writing on achievement and attitudes of seventh and eighth grade students reading two years below grade level. *Reading Improvement, 26,* 290–297.

Ingersoll, B. (1988). *Your hyperactive child.* New York: Doubleday.

Jadad, A. R., Boyle, M., & Cunningham, C. (1999). *Treatment of attention deficit/hyperactivity disorder: Evidence Report/Technology Assessment No. 11* (AHRQ Publication No. 00-E005). Rockville, MD: Agency for Health Care Research and Quality.

Jensen, P. S., Martin, D., & Cantwell, D. P. (1997). Comorbidity in ADHD: Implications for research, practice, and *DSM-IV. Journal of the American Academy of Child and Adolescent Psychiatry, 36,* 1065–1079.

Jensen, P. S., Shertvette, R. R., Zenakis, S. N., & Ritchters, J. (1993). Anxiety and depressive disorders in attention deficit disorder with hyperactivity: New findings. *American Journal of Psychiatry, 150,* 1203–1209.

Johnston, C. (2002). The impact of attention deficit hyperactivity disorder on social and vocational functioning in adults. In P. S. Jensen & J. R. Cooper (Eds.), *Attention deficit hyperactivity disorder: State of the science, best practices* (pp. 1–21). Kingston, NJ: Civic Research Institute.

Klein, R. G., Abikoff, H., Klass, E., Ganeles, D., Seese, L. M., & Pollack, S. (1997). Clinical efficacy of methylphenidate in conduct disorder with and without attention deficit hyperactivity disorder. *Archives of General Psychiatry, 54,* 1073–1080.

Mannuzza, S., Klein, R. G., Bessler, A., Malloy, P., & LaPadula, M. (1998). Adult psychiatric status of hyperactive boys as grown up. *American Journal of Psychiatry, 155,* 493–498.

Manzo, K. K., & Zehr, M. A. (1998). Take note. *Education Week, 18*(3), 3.

McInerney, M., Reeve, A., & Kane, M. B. (1995). *Synthesizing and verifying effective practices for children and youth with attention deficit disorder.* Washington, DC: Chesapeake Institute.

MTA Cooperative Group. (1999a). Fourteen-month randomized clinical trial of treatment strategies for attention-deficit hyperactivity disorder. *Archives of General Psychiatry, 56,* 1073–1086.

MTA Cooperative Group. (1999b). Effects of comorbid anxiety, poverty, session attendance, and community medication on treatment outcome in children with attention deficit/hyperactivity disorder. *Archives of General Psychiatry, 56,* 1088–1096.

National Institute of Mental Health. (1999). *Questions and answers: NIMH multimodal treatment study of children with ADHD.* Bethesda, MD: Author.

National Institute of Mental Health. (2000). *NIMH research on treatment for attention deficit hyperactivity disorder (ADHD): The multimodal treatment study—questions and answers.* Retrieved January 12, 2007, from www.nimh.nih.gov/events/mtaqa.cfm

National Institute of Mental Health. (2006). *Attention deficit hyperactivity disorder* (NIH) Publication No. 3572). Bethesda, MD: U.S. Department of Health and Human Services.

National Dissemination Center for Children with Disabilities. (2004). *Attention-deficit/hyperactivity disorder.* Retrieved April 30, 2007, from http://www.nichcy.org/pubs/factshe/fs14txt.htm

Neuwirth, S. (1994). *Attention deficit hyperactivity disorder* (NIH Publication No. 96-3572). Bethesda, MD: National Institutes of Health.

Olsen, J. (2003). *Handwriting without tears.* Retrieved May 23, 2003, from http://hwtears.com

"OSEP Letter to Michel Williams." (1994, March 14). *21 Individuals with Disabilities Education Law Report 73.*

Osman, B. B. (2000). Learning disabilities and the risk of psychiatric disorders in children and adolescents. In L. Greenhill (Ed.), *Learning disabilities in children with a psychiatric disorder* (pp. 33–57). Washington, DC: American Psychiatric Association.

Pastor, P. N., & Reuben, C. A. (2002). Attention deficit disorder and learning disability: United States, 1997–98. *Vital Health Stat, 10*(206).

Pelham W. E., & Fabiano, G. (2001). Behavior modification. *Child and Adolescent Psychiatry Clinics of North America, 9*(3), 671–688.

Pelham, W. E., Jr., Gnagy, E. M., Greenslade, K. E., & Milich, R. (1992). Teacher ratings of DSM-III-R symptoms for the disruptive behavior disorders. *Journal of the American Academy of Child and Adolescent Psychiatry, 31,* 210–218.

Pelham, W. E., & Hoza, B. (1996). Intensive treatment: A summer treatment program for children with ADHD. In E. Hibbs & H. Jensen (Eds.), *Psychosocial treatment for child and adolescent disorders: Empirically based strategies for clinical practice* (pp. 311–340). New York: American Psychological Association.

Pelham, W. E., Wheeler, T., & Chronis, A. (1998). Empirically supported psychosocial treatments for attention deficit hyperactivity disorder. *Journal of Clinical Child Psychology, 27,* 190–205.

Pierangelo, R., & Giuliani, G. (2006). *Learning disabilities: A practical approach to foundations, assessment, diagnosis and teaching.* Needham Heights, MA: Allyn and Bacon.

Pierangelo, R., & Giuliani, G. (2007). *The educator's diagnostic manual of disabilities and disorders (EDM).* San Francisco: Jossey Bass.

Rabiner, D. (2006). *Educational rights for children with ADHD.* Retrieved April 30, 2007, from http://www.helpforadd.com/educational-rights/

Rapport, M. D., Stoner, G., & Jones, J. T. (1986). Comparing classroom and clinic measures of attention deficit disorder: Differential, idiosyncratic, and dose-response effects of methylphenidate. *Journal of Counseling and Clinical Psychology, 54,* 334–341.

Robelia, B. (1997). Tips for working with ADHD students of all ages. *Journal of Experimental Education, 20*(1), 51–53.

Robin, A. (1998). *ADHD in adolescents: Diagnosis and treatment.* New York: Guilford Press.

Schiller, E. (1996). Educating children with attention deficit disorder. *Our Children, 22*(2), 32–33.

Scruggs, T. E., & Mastropieri, M. A. (2000). The effectiveness of mnemonic instruction for students with learning and behavior problems: An update and research synthesis. *Journal of Behavioral Education, 10*(2/3), 163–173.

Shaffer, D., Gould, M. S., Fisher, P., Trautment, P., Moreau, D., Kleinman, M., et al. (1996). Psychiatric diagnosis in child and adolescent suicide. *Archives of General Psychiatry, 53,* 339–348.

Slavin, R. E. (2002). *Education psychology: Theory into practice.* Boston, MA: Allyn and Bacon.

Swanson, J. M. (1992). *School-based assessments and interventions for ADHD students.* Irvine, CA: K. C. Publishing.

Todd, A. W., Horner, R. H., Sugai, G., & Sprague, J. R. (1999). Effective behavior support: Strengthening school-wide systems through a team-based approach. *Effective School Practices, 17*(4), 23–37.

U.S. Department of Education. (2004). *Teaching children with attention deficit hyperactivity disorder: Instructional strategies and practices.* Washington, DC: U.S. Office of Special Education Programs.

U.S. Department of Health and Human Services. (1999). *Mental health: A report of the surgeon general.* Washington, DC: Author.

Wagner, M., & Blackorby, J. (2002). *Disability profiles of elementary and middle school students with disabilities.* Menlo Park, CA: SRI International.

Waslick, B., & Greenhill, L. (1997). Attention-deficit/hyperactivity disorder. In J. M. Weiner (Ed.), *Textbook of child and adolescent psychiatry* (2nd ed., pp. 389–410). Washington, DC: American Academy of Child and Adolescent Psychiatry, American Psychiatric Press.

Wolraich, M. L., Hannah, J. N., Pinock, T. Y., Baumgaertel, A., & Brown, J. (1996). Comparison of diagnostic criteria for attention-deficit hyperactivity disorder in a county-wide sample. *Journal of the American Academy of Child and Adolescent Psychiatry, 35,* 319–324.

Zametkin, A. J., & Ernst, M. (1999). Current concepts: Problems in the management of attention-deficit/hyperactivity disorder. *New England Journal of Medicine, 340*(1), 40–46.

Zentall, S. S. (1993). Research on the educational implications of attention deficit hyperactivity disorder. *Exceptional Children, 60,* 143–153.

Index